Other books by Brett Novick

Beyond the Behavior Contract: A Practical Approach to Dealing with Challenging Student Behaviors

The Balanced Child: Teaching Children and Students the Gifts of Social Skills

The Likable, Effective and Productive Educator: Being the Best You Can Be as an Educator

Parents and Teachers Working Together: Addressing School's Most Vital Stakeholders

THE ANGRY CHILD

THE ANGRY CHILD

What Parents, Schools, and Society Can Do

Brett Novick

ROWMAN & LITTLEFIELD
Lanham • Boulder • New York • London

Published by Rowman & Littlefield
An imprint of The Rowman & Littlefield Publishing Group, Inc.
4501 Forbes Boulevard, Suite 200, Lanham, Maryland 20706
www.rowman.com

6 Tinworth Street, London SE11 5AL

British Library Cataloguing in Publication Information Available

Library of Congress Cataloging-in-Publication Data Available

978-1-4758-4879-3 (cloth)
978-1-4758-4880-9 (electronic)

CONTENTS

ACKNOWLEDGMENTS

I was lucky that I met the right mentors and teachers at the right moment.

—James Levine

I would like to dedicate this book to my late father, Dr. William Novick, who taught me how to be a father. To my parents who both taught me the importance of hard work and values. My wife, Darla who teaches me each and every day how to be a better man, parent, and spouse. My children Billy, Samantha, who give me hope for the future generation with pride. Also, to the many people that I have had the honor of working with over the years who have taught me so very much. To Brian Woodruff, whose creative spirit inspired me and so many other people. Please know, it has been an honor to be allowed to play a small part in their lives. The many mentors who in both education and life inspired me in every aspect of my life. Thank you to all.

PREFACE

Anybody can become angry—that is easy, but to be angry with the right person and to the right degree, and at the right time, and for the right purpose, and in the right way—that is not within everybody's power and is not easy.

—Aristotle

Turn on the television and you will likely see images of war: civilians carried away from war zones on stretchers and heavily clad soldiers with assault rifles going with surgical precision from building to building, room to room, with the barrel of a weapon leading the way. Those who do make it out have a look of utter fear in their eyes as they run for their lives from the very place that once was a bastion of safety and security.

But this is no war zone. Far from it: It is a public school, and the children are running from the explosive violence of a peer who has turned against them in the most horrifying of ways. It is the same story, over and over: A youth sees school as the place to make a most profound statement of anger, rage, and hate, sacrificing their peers in a murderous rampage as their testament.

These images, which seemingly originated with Columbine two decades ago, have repeated themselves in an ever-voracious cycle. These incidents have not slowed down, nor do they show any signs of doing so. It seems that each perpetrator seems more hell-bent on outdoing the last, each trying to outdo the other in some sick, distorted statement of anger, bitterness, and hatred. But in this anger, what are they trying to say? Why are they saying it? Is there something we can learn from the anger—or, better yet, can we discover why are they so enraged *now*, before evermore anger explodes?

We can discuss gun rights and laws in town halls, the federal government, and social media. Certainly, these forums are a necessary framework for potential change, but more often these debates seem to be a lightning rod for those on both sides sides to dig their heels in. It seems this issue has become one of those "not to discuss" subject areas, joining abortion, politics, and religion. For these reasons, it has become a seemingly intractable problem, and this book will not focus on the surrounding political issues, instead focusing on the root causes of the anger of children in this upcoming generation—and what we can possibly do about it.

These questions in themselves may help solve one part of what is a systemic and complex problem. It is easy to point to one particular issue and state that this is the cause of the rage and the solution should be found in one magic panacea that will quench the fires of anger in our youth. Yet if we take this over-simplistic approach, we fail to recognize that the causes of and solutions for anger in the next generation may be just as multifaceted as the origins of this complex emotion itself. It is also potentially shortsighted, ineffective, and even dangerous to look for a quick fix in a world hoping for the instant gratification of an easy answer.

So, where does the answer lie: in parenting, social media, technology, media focus, schooling, peer influence? Perhaps it is all of these, in varying degrees, and must be treated as such. It may take every tool in society's eclectic tool belt to make inroads into the burgeoning problem of anger in our youth. It will take all we have to stem that growing tide of unrest.

This book, then, will look into what we can do to teach our children that anger is not, in itself, a bad emotion. Rather, it is an emotion that, properly harnessed, can provide them with the assertiveness and boundaries necessary to succeed in a frenetic and dynamic world. It can furnish the catalyst and fuel to get things done and pick them up when they are feeling sorry for themselves. But anger is often complex, partnering with other emotions that children (and adults, for that matter) may not be fully aware of unless it is distilled to its most basic nature.

This book will also look at how parents can bolster their parenting skills to help children learn how to handle anger and conflict in an effective manner. In this vein, we will look at how keeping youth from taking responsibility, or fully comprehending the consequences, of their actions often leads to escalating anger and irritation—the very consequence that parents and society are trying to avoid.

We will also spend time looking at the realm of public education, learning how a curriculum that does not teach conflict resolution and appropriate emotional expression has children prepared to take any standardized test but falls short in preparing them for a world that requires relationships with others in every necessary facet of life.

Finally, we will look at social media and technology: the vast uncharted and untamed virtual wilderness of youth, a land where anger and cyberbullying run amok to metastasize and grow unchecked. We will see how technology and social media can be either an incredible educational tool, or a devastating weapon that stunts the growth, self-esteem, and development of youth and learn how we can grow the former without inadvertently incubating the latter.

It is important to realize that anger is complex, and when we dissect it we find that it is the outgrowth of many other negative emotions. It is a combination of sadness, fear, frustration, anxiety, lack of control, poor self-esteem, and a host of other ill-gotten feelings. All of these emotions bleed together like watercolors to create the dark and stormy anger that rains down on our unprepared youth.

I

THE STORM ON THE HORIZON

The Elements of Anger and Youth

Angry people want you to see how powerful they are. Loving people want you to see how powerful you are.

—Chief Red Eagle

"No, you are not going to Johnny's house to play," Michael's mother states firmly despite his begging and pleading otherwise. His mother attempts to explain that he has not done his chores or his homework, and that these tasks are not unreasonable for his role as an eight-year-old in the their home.

Michael attempts to negotiate with his mother that he will do all that is expected of him when he gets home from Johnny's house. He does so in his usual raised voice that is a mix of contempt, demand, and questioning. He and his mother go back and forth, debating like two seasoned attorneys in a major court case.

After several minutes of a back-and-forth game of strategic chess, Michael's mother has had enough: "No, you are not going to Johnny's house to play today! That is it! End of story!" With that statement comes a barrage of profanity that would make a truck driver blush from the mouth of this eight-year-old. Michael becomes an emotional tornado as he throws items and destroys the carefully manicured living room yet again.

ARE OUR KIDS MORE ANGRY NOW?

According to a 2012 study by Harvard Medical School, one in twelve teens has what can be classified as an anger disorder.[1] In 2008 the UK's Mental Health Foundation released a report about problematic anger titled, *Boiling Point*, noting that among those polled 64 percent said that the world is indeed becoming an angrier place. Yet, in the same report, fewer than one in seven (13 percent) of those who said they have trouble controlling their anger, have actively sought help for their anger problems. Worse yet, 58 percent of respondents said they didn't know where to seek help with an anger problem even if they wanted to do so.[2]

It does not help that anger spreads like wildfire in the dry tinder of the internet. In fact, a 2013 study by Rui Fan and colleagues determined that the emotion of anger goes viral online more often than feelings like sorrow or happiness. They grouped the emotions of more than 70 million posts on a social-networking site in China and observed which emotions were most often shared. The data noted that while happy posts were shared by those who were closely related, angry posts were shared by those removed from the original person's contacts. Rui and colleagues note that anger is likely the most viral (rapidly spreading) emotion on the web.[3]

In this book I could quote many hundreds of studies and reams of statistics that indicate the uptick of anger and aggression in recent years. Yet numbers don't tell us what to do, nor does the increasing diagnosis of ADHD or the broad spectrum of anger disorders. They just place a label on what we already know: Anger is the constant background music that drones in modern society. Labels and multitudes of studies cannot act as a Band-Aid to begin to fix what is happening in the next generation and perhaps those to come after. Stats tell us only numbers: not a how, not a why, nor answers to the difficult questions that we as a society must face head-on.

INABILITY TO FACE REJECTION OR CONSEQUENCES

As parents, some of us attempt to insulate our children from potential consequences or rejection. It is hard to see our children struggle, become upset, fail, or be hurt in any way. Yet that failure, and a small degree of hardship, are precisely the necessary catalyst a child—or an adult, for that matter—needs to grow.

Like it or not, being rejected and failing are part of growing up. These experiences teach children to redirect their emotional and social compass slightly, build their frustration tolerance, and try again. When children do not experience failure, rejection, or the natural consequences of poor choices, they ultimately end up learning the hard way as adolescents or young adults in the rough-and-tumble real world. Many react in anger because they have developed a degree of entitlement and learned that no one should disrupt the bubble of comfort built around them since birth.

Take, for instance, the mentality that everyone should earn a trophy for participation in an activity or sport. In practice, it sounds like a kind gesture: Everyone is recognized, everyone is happy, and everyone succeeds. But what happens when the real world rears its ugly head—a world in which one person is often rewarded for his or her efforts and others are largely left out? Do these individuals react in anger and self-pity? Do they try again harder? Do they quit? Or do they realign their compass, note what they may improve upon, and muster the strength to go in another direction?

Let's use another example: If a child is rejected on the playground, what does she do? She can continue to try to force herself upon the children who have rejected her or she can seek the company of others on the playground who may accept her more readily. Facing this kind of rejection can teach children how to handle it, or it can teach them to crumple into flaming balls of anger, frustration, and self-pity. A certain degree of consequence exercises children's social muscles, hence preparing them for a world to which they must adapt themselves (and not the other way around).

HANDICAPPED SOCIAL SKILLS

Today's kids are drawn to the glow of a smartphone screen like moths to a flame. This is the contemporary contradiction of modern communication: socializing with more people, but with less quality in those communications. Children now have a far greater scope of peers they can, or do, interact with, yet, at the very same time, those conversations are more often shallow, hollow, and incomplete.

At issue is the part of interaction that modern exchanges are sorely lacking: the full experience of face-to-face communication. Research indicates that only 7 percent of any message is conveyed through our actual words; 38 percent is conveyed through how we phrase things, and a full 55 percent is conveyed through our body language.[4]

This means that our children are neither practicing nor developing more than 50 percent of the necessary elements for accurate communication. Without the ability to understand body language or the way things are phrased, they misunderstand, misread, or otherwise misinterpret conversations between themselves and others. It is like trying to hear a quiet conversation in a loud room, getting only every other word and attempting to piece together what is being said.

IS SOCIAL MEDIA FUELING ANGER?

It takes only a few minutes on any social media website to recognize that anger and hatred have invaded the internet. Adults "unfriending" each other over points of view and debates that attack one's very soul and character are prevalent in every social media channel. Many of these adult matters filter down to the ears of children as well.

In 2018, the Associated Press–NORC Center for Public Affairs Research determined that "76 percent of 13- to 17-year-olds use Instagram, 75 percent use Snapchat, 66 percent use Facebook, 47 percent use Twitter, and fewer than 30 percent use Tumblr, Twitch, or LinkedIn."[5] A 2009 Finnish study "of 5,516 adolescents that found 10 percent of the boys had been victims, 10 percent had bullied, and 10 percent had witnessed cyberbullying. Among girls, the figures were slightly higher: 11 percent, 9 percent, and 16 percent, respectively."[6]

This is not to mention that we are creating a generation of perpetually cranky children/adolescents. In a study published in the *Journal of Youth Studies*, nine hundred adolescents in Great Britain between the ages of twelve and fifteen were interviewed; researchers found that one-fifth of the teens said they "almost always" wake up during the night and log in to social media.[7]

The result? A generation of children and teenagers who are always on the emotional edge of sleep deprivation and emotional irritation. This is backed up by a study in the *Journal of Violence*, where researchers at Iowa State University found evidence that lack of sleep can be a catalyst for aggression and anger.[8] The researchers were able to draw a further correlation between the influence of a lack of restful sleep on impulsivity and how individuals respond to what they deem as threats.

THE LOSS OF FLUENCY IN NONVERBAL COMMUNICATION CREATES ANGRY AND FRUSTRATED KIDS

With children using technology as the primary way of interacting with each other, the importance of the respective nonverbal elements is placed on the back burner. So the question becomes: Is a text or media post sarcastic, serious, funny, insulting, hostile, or complimentary? This is all up for interpretation, and children—and many adults—are notoriously bad at interpreting these interactions.

How bad? According to some research, even close friends and married couples are able to accurately determine the intentions or feelings of those close to them only 35 percent of the time on average. "Almost no one ever scores higher than 60 percent (in this test)," report psychologists William Ickes and Marianne Mast, founders of empathic accuracy studies at the University of Texas at Arlington.[9] What of children who do not have the wisdom of a lifetime of conversational and social skills? They certainly must score even lower in interpreting the texts and social media posts of their peers.

What about the hundreds of brief texts, posts, or conversations that are especially obscure in their intention? Children, much like adults, tend to look toward the negative end of clouded communication and dialogue. Think about the worst thing your parent said to you as a child or the most hurtful statement a peer made to you in middle school. Now shift gears and think of the kindest comment made to you by your parents or peers. Which is easier to recall?

If you are like most of us, you will tend to quickly recall the negative statements, and they will tend to stick in your head the longest. After analyzing some twelve thousand diary entries, Dr. Teresa M. Amabile, director of research at Harvard Business School, found that "the negative effect of a setback at work on happiness was more than twice as strong as the positive effect of an event that signaled progress. And the power of a setback to increase frustration is over three times as strong as the power of progress to decrease frustration."[10] Thus, the power of negativity tends to be a far greater magnet than the pull of positive interactions.

Clearly, children are going to continue to utilize social media as their primary means of communication. It will likely become even more ingrained in childhood social life with each successive year of this next generation. So how do we ensure that they use this medium in a manner that provides clear dialogue?

- *Have children use technology as it is intended:* Social media platforms are best used to transmit small bits of messages to another person. As a result, emotional and complicated relationship issues are often misconstrued if used in this medium. Encourage children to use voice communication to practice conflict resolution and conversational skills.
- *Have youth use texts for informational, not relational, communication:* Like social media, texts are good for conveying purely informational messages. Relational information cannot be transmitted—or understood—accurately in the black-and-white of a text message. Therefore, use face-to-face conversation for socialization and leave technology to convey information.
- *Ask questions, explore, and clarify:* Because messages sent using social media and other technology can be so difficult to interpret accurately, encourage children to ask questions, explore, and clarify. This will help them avoid jumping to an angry conclusion and an ensuing tirade that they may later regret.
- *Stop and think:* It is all too easy for children to react to a post with a simple type, swipe, and send. Once gone, however, that digital dialogue can't be taken back. Encourage children to stop and think before sending any correspondence via the internet.

ARE VIDEO GAMES FUELING ANGER?

In the 1970s and 1980s, when video games first made a major splash in the world of children and teens, the video games themselves were vastly different. It is true that they often had a subtle suggestion of violence, but they were largely cartoonish, unrealistic pixels.

Video games today have scripts and graphics that are more akin to a full-length feature film than the juvenile games of years ago. Additionally, where once two people played shoulder to shoulder, right next to each other, now youth use the internet to play games with a large network of people and with little, or no, face-to-face contact.

So the question remains: Do video games really cause violence? The verdict is largely out, and the answer differs based on who you talk to. What these games may create, however, is a decreased sensitivity to empathy and guilt regarding activities that mirror violence. In other words, the experience of virtual violence may harden youth to activities involving actual violence.

Studies have found that repeated violent video game playing leads to emotional desensitization with regard to future video game playing experiences. Put another way, video games may dull players' sense of empathy to the fictional characters they dispose of in massive numbers in video games.[11] Other research notes that "exposure to violent video games increases aggressive thoughts, angry feelings, physiological arousal and aggressive behaviors, and decreases the likelihood of helpful or altruistic behaviors."[12]

SOCIETY HAS IT TOO EASY

A long time ago, our ancestors were hunters. This meant that they had to be fast to be able to eat or they would starve (or be eaten by something else). It also meant that they had to use anger, adrenaline, and anything they had to survive from minute to minute. The skills of coordination, quick thinking, and rapid action were all necessary components of life for continuance as a species.

This survival switch is often referred to as the fight-or-flight instinct. All of us—children and adults alike—have this instinct still buried deep within us. Those neurological programs and routines that we once used for survival, food, and shelter are now dispatched at inappropriate times as unfocused anger. Worse yet, when we are in that fight-or-flight mode, the adrenaline forces our blood and energy to our limbs (for running or fighting) and away from our brain (for thinking).[13] This is why people in the fog of rage experience a certain type of tunnel vision that prevents them from thinking clearly or coming up with proactive solutions to a problem.

KIDS CANNOT BE KIDS

In today's fast-paced world, children are barraged with more information than ever before. The data is often unfiltered, inappropriate, or even unreliable. Many television shows, movies, and even websites have adult-oriented humor and themes that are subtly directed at children.

As a result, children are often subjected to material they are not prepared to handle, including violence and other content that is inappropriate for their development. This creates children who are attempting to be adults before they are ready and indeed it has become a badge of honor for children to act like adults before their time.

LESS ATTENTION = MORE FRUSTRATION AND ANGER

Dr. Wei Bao, assistant professor of epidemiology at the University of Iowa College of Public Health, and his colleagues reviewed data from the National Health Interview Survey between 1997 and 2017, finding that during that time, the incidence of attention deficit hyperactivity disorder (ADHD) increased from 9 percent to 14 percent in boys and from 3 percent to 6 percent in girls. When they further looked at subgroups based on income, race, and geographic location, they found these numbers were also significantly higher in each demographic.[14]

How does this relate to increased anger in children? As adults, many of us adopt the simple proactive strategy of "ready, set, go" in our lives; that is, we ready ourselves for what we want to do, we set ourselves in that direction, we develop a vision to get there, and then we attempt to do it. In between these choices comes thinking about the consequences of our potential actions on ourselves and others and how to get what we want done within the confines of rules and society.

Those with ADHD sometimes do things a little differently. Children who have ADHD tend to mix up these directions and instead "go, ready, set"; that is, they do it, and then think about the consequences after. This leads to frustration as they have to try to restrain their impulses or deal with the consequence of handling something after they have already behaved in a manner that often leads to both anger and frustration.

INCREASED EXPECTATIONS = LOWER FRUSTRATION TOLERANCE

As the world gets ever smaller and more competitive, so does our need to feel that our children can compete within the world market at an earlier and earlier age. A recent study published in the *Psychological Bulletin Journal* looked at forty thousand college students in the United States, England, and Canada to see what their attitudes were in terms of the need for perfection. The study found a disturbing trend: a 33 percent surge in these late adolescents feeling the need to "be perfect" to win approval from their parents, friends, and society in general. Additionally, the research found that these teens tended to have the same impossibly lofty standards for others, treating those who didn't reach that level with hostility and disdain. [15]

CHILDREN FEEL LESS IN CONTROL AND MORE CONTROLLED

We all tend to feel less angry and frustrated when we believe we control our fate and destiny and that no one else has the power to change this. If we feel that someone else is in command of our lives, we become anxious, resentful, and ultimately angry.

Yet that lack of control is precisely what children today are feeling and indicating. In 2010, psychology professor Jean Twenge and her colleagues at San Diego State University looked at whether today's children perceive they are in control of their fate or whether they believe factors external to themselves are responsible for their ultimate destiny. More than 80 percent of youth feel less in control of their lives than adolsecents did only a generation earlier. [16]

Without control, there is a lack of responsibility. With a lack of responsibility comes an inability to acknowledge and address the problems of conflict, discord, and anger that children today feel on a regular basis. In a world in which the "buck is passed," our children don't know how to handle it when "the buck stops with them."

2

PARENTING THE ANGRY CHILD

Every child senses, with all the horse sense that's in him, that any parent is angry inside when children misbehave and they dread more the anger that is rarely or never expressed openly, wondering how awful it may be.

—Benjamin Spock, MD

Mary decides to make a quick, unscheduled detour to her local convenience store for a cup of coffee. She drives around the lot for what seems like an eternity until she finds an empty space. She has a busy day ahead and a lot to cross off the to-do list on her smartphone.

Mary hastily turns to the backseat and says to her daughter, "Abigail, listen, mommy is really tired and needs a cup of coffee. I am going to go in and get some coffee." Six-year-old Abigail whines to her mother, "Mommy, I want some candy when we go in pleeease!" Mary quickly cuts Abigail off: "No, I don't have enough money for candy, and besides, you don't need that junk. It will rot your teeth out of your head!"

Mary rushes out of the cold winter's chill and into the convenience store with Abigail in tow. As Mary looks around the store she remembers that she needs the essentials—bread, eggs, and milk—and begins to hunt down each of these items. Meanwhile, out of the corner of her eye, she sees Abigail reaching for a fistful of candy bars.

Mary sternly reminds Abigail, "I said no candy bars!" Just as Mary stuffs the loaf of bread under her arm and begins to pour her cup o' joe, she notices Abigail lying on the ground in a heap, crying, screaming, and pounding the ground, repeating over and over again, "I want my candy bars! You promised me candy! I want my candy bars!"

Mary becomes worried and embarrassed that Abigail is making such a scene, as many of her friends frequent this convenience store. Mary now starts to beg and plead, as she too stomps and screams: "Abigail please get off the floor!" After a few moments of a mommy tantrum, Mary says, "Fine! Just get the darn candy bar!"

THE BEGINNING IS A VERY GOOD PLACE TO START

When you look at children who have anger issues, you will notice that many of these children at a young age had difficulty self-soothing. That is, even as infants they often had trouble getting to sleep, staying asleep, or finding means to calm themselves independently. They may have been labeled "fussy" or "colicky" babies.

Flash forward to the future. As these children begin to grow, they may have the same challenges with soothing their anxiety—but this anxiety now presents itself in the form of anger.

ROUTINE = SAFETY

The easiest way to generate distrust, anxiety, and anger in a young child is to not provide a constant and consistent routine. Regardless of their age, children rapidly equate an inconsistent routine and a lack of predictability with danger. This means that having consistent morning, afternoon, evening, and bedtime routines each night is a source of comfort. In a world that can often be chaotic and unpredictable, the world of home must be the bedrock of that consistency.

A typical schedule may look like this:

- Get up around at 7:00 a.m.
- Out of bed by 7:30 a.m.
- Bathroom and brushing teeth by 7:45 a.m.
- Breakfast and in the car by 8:15 a.m.
- Arrival at daycare/preschool/school by 8:30 a.m.
- Pickup from daycare/preschool/school by 4:30 p.m.

- Free/play time between 4:30 and 5:00 p.m.
- Dinner at 5:15 p.m.
- Bath around 6:30 p.m.
- In bed by 8:00 p.m.
- Quiet/asleep by 8:30 p.m. [1]

Why Is Routine So Important?

How does the establishment of a routine correlate with anger and behavioral issues? Well, first let's think about why children misbehave. Often it is to get something or to gain control and influence in their little world. Whether it is a two-year-old having a temper tantrum or a seventeen-year-old arguing about why he or she should have keys to the car, the goal of the behavior is much the same—to gain some level of control.

Routine provides the belief that the world is predictable and safe even when you have little to no control over it. It assures young children that they do, in fact, have some control in a big and scary world. Control is routine and routine is control.

HOW ARE YOU WATERING THE GARDEN OF ATTENTION?

If you wanted to grow a flower garden, what would you do? One would imagine you would carefully feed and water the flowers to ensure their growth. You would vigilantly keep insects off the flowers, fertilize, and carefully prune the foliage to ensure that your roses, sunflowers, and lilies grew to their maximum potential.

Now, on the flip side, you would give dramatically less attention to those weeds that multiply and try to choke out your flowers. You would pull them out, starve them of food and water in hopes that they would simply wither away. However, if you decided that you wanted to grow those much faster-growing and invasive weeds, you could just give them a little water and fertilizer and they would quickly overtake your beautiful garden.

Growing a child's behavior is no different. If you want to see a behavior grow, feed it. Conversely, if you want to see that action wither, ignore it. Simple, right? However, if a child seeks attention, it will generally more easily grow and flourish in the soil of negative behaviors than in what are the "expected" positive ones.

If you have ever heard the phrase "Children should be seen and not heard," you understand how this concept works. What if, as a child, I want to be seen? Then I must be heard. How can I be most heard? By yelling, screaming, and acting out! I will then be heard, given attention, and the adults will be forced to "hear" only me. My parents and others in authority will have to ignore my younger siblings, their social media, the television, the work they brought home from the office. They will hear only me, loud and clear! They will feed and water my need for negative attention with undivided attention.

Do . . . Don't Threaten, Don't Talk, Don't Scream

Often when children are angry and having a tantrum, parents make veiled threats in a vain attempt to get them to stop doing what they are doing. We beg, we plead, we threaten—and in the end these attempts all fall on deaf ears. They are nothing more than empty words that the child comes to expect as such.

If you are going to apply a consequence, then do it. Make sure your limits are clear and appropriate, and then enforce them. Don't continue to belabor the point and talk about what you are going to do. Your words are like ammunition; you only have a set amount, and when you are out you are powerless. The more talking you do, the more powerless you become.

ARE YOU AN OUT-OF-CONTROL PILOT?

Let's imagine for a moment that you are deathly afraid to fly in an airplane (this may not be difficult if you, in fact, are). You get on the airplane and look around, you listen for every unusual sound that may indicate a defective aircraft, and you wring your hands in anxious worry. This will be the longest few hours of your life, and each minute will seem like a proverbial lifetime.

But why? The answer lies mostly in the fact that you cannot control the airplane that you are in. You must depend solely on faith and the expertise of the pilot. You are simply a helpless soul sitting in the cabin and are at the mercy of the crew in the cockpit. What if you were told that the pilot and the crew were inexperienced? What if you knew this was the pilot's first flight as a captain? What if you thought the plane had some major structural defect that had been only recently repaired? What if, instead of that usual calm and soothing pilot voice, you detected a hint of fear or lack of confidence in the pilot's tone? Would this change your level of fear and anxiety?

Likely it would. If those who control your fate are not certain, competent, or reassuring, you are likely respond with a mixture of anxiety, fear, and anger. Children are no different. If children sense that their "parental pilot" does not know what course to steer the family, they will react with a mix of frustration, anger, and fear. Are you a parental pilot who makes them feel reassured and safe? Are you a parental pilot they can count on to get them safely through their turbulent childhood to a meaningful destination?

DO YOU CALL 911 FOR EVERYTHING?

Most of us guide our lives by a set of priorities. When something comes up, we ask ourselves: To what degree is this important, based upon my priorities and values? If family is your most important priority, then everything else takes a back seat in your decision making. If something else (i.e., work, sports, technology) is more vital, this is apparent in your choices as well.

If you have no priorities and everything is of equal importance and value, then you have an issue. If everything is equal, how do you know what is important? This becomes an overwhelming challenge if you don't have some form of leveling urgency, because you become a parent who always "cries wolf" for every issue, minor or major. More importantly, how do you know what is critical? If one thing is an emergency, then everything becomes an emergency. This creates anxiety, anger, frustration in the household.

Decide what you want to be dominant in terms of your priorities for parenting. Look at what it is you want to put on the top of your list, and use this as your go-to when making choices. The first option should always be the physical and mental safety of your child, but all other choices are a matter of preference and need.

WHAT ARE YOUR PARENTAL PRIORITIES, THEN?

When you decide what your parental priorities are, you can avoid sending inconsistent messages or acting as though everything is a crisis, which leads to families that overreact to even the most minor issues.

Here are some examples:

- *Safety:* The physical and emotional well-being of your children should always be at the top of your priority list. Without safety, you cannot create the atmosphere necessary for the other values to bloom.
- *Integrity:* This is the value you place upon your child, and your family, doing the right thing even when no one is watching. This grows via modeling such behavior.
- *Resilience:* This is the ability to persist despite setbacks, and it is a vital family skill. Children can, and will, face many hardships, large and small. Sheltering them does not provide resilience.
- *Empathy:* This is the ability to try to understand things from another's perspective versus solely from your own. Being able to place yourself in someone else's shoes is key to being able to work as a team, as a family, and in society at large.
- *Creativity:* This is the ability to accomplish goals in an unconventional way (i.e., "thinking outside the box"). Those children who cannot generate the skills of thinking of novel means of handling a problem often become easily "stuck" and frustrated and unable to achieve goals that are not merely "right and wrong."
- *Citizenship:* This is being an active part of your school, religious, and local community and contributing positively. Children must understand that they are a part of a larger fabric of society and community that they must contribute to reciprocally.

THE FACE AND FEAR OF REJECTION

It is an unpleasant fact of life that all children will face rejection at some point—and probably at many points in their life. Rejection is painful, unpleasant, and hurtful. Nothing is more painful to most parents than hearing their children cry when they are rejected by a peer or failing at some important task at which they've tried so diligently. The desire is to wrap our children in a cocoon to protect them from the gravity of these issues.

Yet facing rejection provides one of the most valuable lessons in life: how to take responsibility for our actions and recognize that we will not always succeed in everything the first—or even the second or third—time. Rejection is becoming an ever more pressing issue. These days, rejection can be doled out in a very public and harsh manner via the bullhorn that is social media (more on that later). So inoculating children against rejection is more important now than ever before.

Allow for Failure

When we don't allow for minor failures or rejection, we fail to teach our children to build a tolerance for such rejection. When we vaccinate our children, they are given a mild or weakened version of the illness so that they build immunity in hopes that they will never receive the full brunt of a particular disease.

The question is: Do we do the same for failure? If children are not allowed to experience the mild sting of failure in the protected world of childhood, how will they react in the so-called real world of life, when they are punched by it more harshly? When we instead allow them to experience failure and rejection, children learn that if they do not receive instant gratification for a task, they should move on to develop the skills necessary to succeed.

DON'T STEP IN TOO QUICKLY

Be careful not to step in too quickly to help children facing a problem. Let them try to solve the little issues and puzzles in life themselves first.

This helps them build a tolerance for frustration or learn important problem-solving skills.

A simple rule of thumb is: Don't do for children what they are capable of doing themselves. That seems very simple, but when we are in a rush and make the bed for them, run to the grocery store to buy something they forgot, or don't allow them to sulk and not get on with our own day, we often step in to do things for them instead of allowing them to do it, and experience it, themselves.

TEACH CHILDREN TO SEPARATE FAILING FROM BEING A FAILURE

We have all failed at something—numerous things, in fact. What generally keeps us afloat and moving in the right direction is recognizing that while we may not have succeeded in an activity, that failure is not who we are, our entirety, or a person. In other words, we failed at accomplishing the activity, we did not fail as a person.

For instance, as an adult, you may recognize that you are not the best handyman. Maybe you have even failed at certain aspects of home improvement. That being said, you are not a failure as a person because of your weakness in this particular skill. If someone asked, you would be able to give a balanced account of your successes in other areas as well the ones in which you could better yourself.

Children, who are are more egocentric little beings, may say, "I am a failure; I am good at nothing." A parent's natural instinct is to fill that void of confidence with positive statements such as "You are not a failure; you are amazing; we love you." The trouble is that the child begins to constantly look to others—namely, the adults in charge—as the source (or sources) of control for their self-esteem and the regulation of their emotions.

Teaching children to find positive attributes in themselves when they have failed at something is important; otherwise they will always seek confidence and acceptance through others outside themselves. This can be a dangerous proposition in the unpredictable world of relationships—as a child and as an adult.

So what do we do when our children are down on themselves and seek adult approval to bolster their self-esteem? We can require they build confidence, and believe it, for themselves and not look to others to do what they ultimately must do for themselves. For instance, we can ask:

- What are three things you are good at?
- What are three traits you like about yourself?
- What are three things you can do to make this problem better?

WHOSE BED IS IT, ANYWAY?

Sometimes we step in and try to solve problems too quickly or to our own satisfaction. When we do this, however, we teach children not to rely on themselves or their abilities, in the long run, thus creating greater frustration and diminished self-esteem. We teach them, in subtle ways, that they are simply not good enough.

Let's take that earlier example of making the bed, a very common childhood chore. When you remake the beds in a way that is more to your liking, what are you telling your children? You are telling them that they do not do it *right*. They then believe that they *cannot* do it rather than that you are improving upon their attempts. This lowers their ability to accept frustration, criticism, and challenge, and this can carry on throughout their lives.

ADULTS ARE NOT MIND READERS

Sometimes angry children resort to shutting down. They fold their arms, stomp their feet, and give the silent treatment. Parents are tempted to play a game of one hundred questions to determine what is wrong: What are you angry about? Are you mad at me? What do you need?

Imagine if you tried this strategy with your supervisor, making him or her try to guess what is wrong with you. You would be out on the street quicker than a flash, looking for another job. It is not your supervisor's job to figure out what you need or want without you offering some potential solutions. You are the employee, and your supervisor is not a psychic nor a mind reader.

The same goes for children: It is not the job of a teacher or a parent to determine what they need to resolve their anger. We can help them try to find a way to do so; however, when we prod them for information we are just feeding a behavior that we don't want: sulking and feeling sorry for themselves.

We cannot feed a child's whims by trying to play a futile guessing game of what is making them angry or disturbed; it wastes our energy and time and does nothing productive. Instead, when they begin to try to consult with us as a means to collaboratively resolve an issue, we should engage and give attention to that valid need.

A SURE WAY TO CREATE SNEAKY CHILDREN

If you want to create sneaky and angry children, yell at them when they make mistakes. If children equate failure and mistakes with punishment and anger, they will lie rather than risk getting yelled at or punished.

Instead, parents should allow children to fail and be there with them in the moment. Use the defeat as a teaching moment and a time of honest appraisal not only of what they did wrong but, more importantly, what they learned to do differently. Discuss with them the mix of feelings that are buried under the anger, which often include anxiety, disappointment, and frustration.

A SECOND WAY TO CREATE SNEAKY CHILDREN

Let's suppose that your child has spilled a glass milk in front of you, or, alternatively, you turn your back for a moment and then notice that same spilled glass of milk. What do you do? Many of us ask the question, "Did you spill that milk?" Of course, the answer to that question is obvious. We know who spilled the milk, so why do we even ask?

A SURE WAY TO CREATE FRUSTRATED, ANGRY CHILDREN WITH LOW SELF-ESTEEM

When you give children choices, make sure they are choices you can live with and that they can understand. The most destructive way to parent is to force "darned if you do, darned if you don't" decisions (also know as a double bind).

A classic example of this situation is when children must choose sides in a parental conflict, such as when the child's parents are divorced. No matter which side the child chooses, the other parent becomes disappointed or even angry. Either choice is a losing one, hence forcing children to make such a choice creates nothing but frustration, anger, guilt, and sadness.

SICK, TIRED, HUNGRY, BORED, UNCOMFORTABLE

When we talk with children, we often expect them to respond like miniature adults. Children, however, are not simply little adults. They have vastly different developmental, emotional, and physical needs than their adult counterparts. This is often overlooked, especially when a seemingly mature or eldest child is concerned.

Children also, unfortunately, have far less ability to read their own thoughts, physical symptoms, and emotions. Have you ever seen a child simply fall apart emotionally? Children are just not able to decipher where or when they are hungry, sick, tired, bored, or otherwise uncomfortable. This may lead to fits of what seems to be unrelated, or untriggered, anger.

In reality, this anger often stems from one issue or a combination of several issues that they are unable to read within themselves; they feel and react to the discomfort, often with frustration, hostility, and anger. Introspection in these areas comes only with age, experience, and wisdom.

THE ROLE OF PARENTING: FOOD, CLOTHING, SHELTER, LOVE, . . . AND A SMARTPHONE?

The job of a parent is fourfold: provide children with food on the table, seasonally appropriate clothing, shelter from the elements, and unconditional love. A parent who provides these necessities and also sprinkles in a fair mix of discipline would be fulfilling the vital job responsibilities for the majority of parenthood.

Children have much higher expectations and set a much anticipated higher bar. They often believe that they are owed other material items that they supposed all their peers have. This "generational entitlement" has always occurred, to one degree or another, in past generations. However, the pressure to keep up with others has been multiplied exponentially with the advent of social media.

Further, children often have unrealistic expectations of their peers. This is primarily because they tend to embellish what their lives and possessions look like on social media. (More on this in a minute.) This creates a situation in which children are trying to keep up with an unrealistic—or outright false—model of what their peers are doing, expecting, and should be getting.

CHILDREN CONTROL NOTHING, ADULTS CONTROL EVERYTHING

One of the best means of controlling anger and anxiety is by having control over your situation and life. Unfortunately, children lack control over most aspects of their lives. Therefore, they hang on to the significant adults in their lives to make decisions.

Adults Control

Adults have a monopoly on most aspects of a child's life. Some of the more important elements include:

- The home they live in and who resides in that home
- Where they are going to go to school and who they will have as their teachers

- How money and financial resources are spent, and on whom

Children Control

Of course, children do have limited control over some aspects of their lives. Children tend to hold on to these small areas within their control like it is all they have—because it is. These include:

- What they are going to wear or not wear
- What they are going to eat or not eat
- When they are going to go to the bathroom or not go
- How they are going to behave or misbehave

Let's look at how these behaviors give rise to anger and conflict:

- "I refuse to wear that. I am only going to wear this."
- "I will only eat chicken nuggets, hot dogs, and pizza."
- At a restaurant:

  - "Do you have to use the bathroom before our food gets here?"
  - Child: "No."
  - Parent: "You sure?"
  - Child: "Yes!"
  - Child (after the food arrives): "I have to use the bathroom right now!"

- Choosing misbehavior (at the store):

  - Child: "Can I get this toy car?"
  - Parent: "No! You cannot; we don't have any money."
  - Child (yelling): "I want the toy car! I want the toy car! I want the toy car!"
  - Parent (embarrased because everyone is looking): "Okay—just be quiet!"
  - Child settles down and immediately and stops the out-of-control, angry behaviors.

CHOICES YOU CAN LIVE WITH

When children are not provided choices, they become angry, anxious, and often desperate. The lack of choices reminds them that they are in control of nothing and that adults control virtually everything.

It becomes a power struggle as they dig in their heels in a desperate attempt to gain control, get what they want, or keep what they have. These power struggles can quickly escalate into all-out battles.

Giving children choices that the adult can live with helps put some of the responsibility and power back in the hands of the child, decreasing anxiety, anger, and frustration for parents and children alike.

HOW TO GIVE CHOICES

Too many choices can be overwhelming. Go to a grocery store and you might see fifty kinds of hot sauce. It can lead to a minor anxiety issue: How do you know which one to buy? What if you buy the wrong one? What if you don't like the taste? Having a lot of choices is not always a good thing.

In fact, in an article in *Psychology Today*, Liraz Margalit notes that having too many choices causes a sort of incapacity to make decisions, which can lead to anxiety, anger, and—in the end—not making any choice at all. In the times when a choice *is* made under these conditions, it is usually accompanied by frustration, anxiety, and irritation.[2]

Let's take a very common example of this issue that often occurs with children. A child comes bounding off the school bus and the following dialogue occurs:

Parent: "How was your day at school?"

Child: "Good."

Parent: "What did you do at school?"

Child: "Nothing."

Asking a more focused and pointed question elicits a more accurate and precise answer; for instance:

> Parent: "I know that you had art today with Ms. Smith. Tell me about the project you worked on."

> Child: "We worked on a mural and . . ." (child goes into detail)

Let's now apply this to the areas children want to control:

- *What they are going to wear:* "You can choose one of these two outfits."
- *What they are going to eat:* "You have to try at least two of the four foods on your plate."
- *When they are going to go to the bathroom:* "You must try to use the bathroom before dinner comes."
- *How they are going to behave:* "We will discuss what you want when you are sitting and ready to listen."

Choices should be:

- *Limited:* Too many choices are overwhelming and cause a shut-down, frustration, or anger.
- *Age-appropriate:* A choice that a child does not understand is not a choice.
- *Possible:* Can you actually give (and live with) the choice?

BE CAREFUL WHAT YOU FIND FUNNY

Often, when children do "adult" things, grown-ups find it funny. Look at the memes or posts on social media and you will find little children emulating adults in their mannerisms or language. However, be cautious what you reinforce. For instance, let's say that your child says a very adult-sounding phrase or profanity, and everyone laughs and/or tells him to say it again because "it's cute"—or, alternatively, they giggle about it later when they think the child is out of earshot. The child sees the adults' reaction and will continue to use these statements in an effort to get the adults to laugh or to get additional attention.

Now, suppose that when the child goes to school, he wants the attention of the teacher and knows he has to compete with the throngs of other children in his class. What will he do? He will apply that same strategy again in another setting. But this time he will receive a very different response and be left genuinely confused, frustrated, and angry that he is now in trouble for the very same behavior that got a laugh at home.

SARCASM GOES OVER LIKE A LEAD BALLOON

If you think about it, many of us use sarcasm in our everyday conversation for humor as well as to get our point across with other adults. The difficulty is that children become frustrated and irritated when we use this language because it is so subtle. Childhood communication, conversely, can cause anger and frustration because children see things very concretely, in black-and-white terms. Therefore, parents should say what they mean and mean what they say.

Let's look at some examples:

Parent: "How many times do I have to tell you not to do that?"

Child: "I don't know. . . maybe four?"

Parent: "Don't get wise with me!"

Child (thinks to self): "She asked me a question, and I gave what I thought was the right answer. Why is she so mad?"

Or, with a younger child:

Parent: "What bugs you?"

Child (taking the question literally): "Flies, bees, mosquitos . . ."

Parent: "Huh?"

ARE YOU A CRACKED OR DEFECTIVE MIRROR?

If you had younger siblings when you were growing up, your parents may have said, "You should know better—you are older!" Parents expect that with age comes maturity and the ability to somehow know better than those who are younger. Age is thus equated with patience, maturity, and improved communication skills.

Yet how many times have you, or another parent or adult you know, been brought to a full-fledged temper tantrum at the hands of a frustrating child—or by or a host of other potential triggers? We all hope that we can act like mature and rational adults all the time, but how often are we not at our best?

We are all susceptible to having a tantrum, regardless of age. The problem is that when we model the behaviors we don't want, our children, in turn, will mirror those same behaviors. It becomes like one of those funhouse mirrors in which the reflected image seems to go on in an infinite cycle.

So don't add fuel to the fire with your own emotional outbursts of anger. Children who see angry, out-of-control adults become angry themselves. The cycle then continues as both child and parent feed off of each other, each escalating the conflict cycle. If you cannot be the calm model of behavior, remove yourself from the situation whenever possible.

RESPECT IS NOT EARNED

As adults we often remind children that, "I am the adult and you are the kid." We remind them, over and over again, that respect is not given—it is earned. However, what if respect is instead a skill that must be taught? What if children have no idea what respect is because, by nature of being children, they are not shown a definition of respect by those who are their elders?

Before respect can be earned it must first be modeled. In other words, if you are expecting your children to display respect, you must first teach them what respect is. Parents teach respect by modeling respect toward their co-parents, strangers, and the children themselves.

Remember, a cracked mirror will generally reflect a damaged image back.

BEING A CHATTERBOX

You may recall, when you were a child, hearing your parents drone on about some life lesson, or about how they had to walk to school "uphill, both ways!" Did you truly listen and learn from that? Most of us did not find any value in those words of wisdom, constant nagging, or long-winded lectures about what we did wrong or what parental rule we broke.

So when you are talking with angry children, remember this: If steam is coming from their ears—like those old cartoon characters whose anger was depicted metaphorically with steam coming out of their ears (often accompanied by the loud whistle of a tea kettle)—very little is getting into their brains. Conserve your words and energy; instead, focus on your actions.

Think of yourself as a police officer who has just pulled over a driver for exceeding the speed limit. Does the officer come running out of his car and go on a long, screaming tirade about how the driver is some kind of maniac? Does he drone on and on about how the driver is irresponsible and stupid? No. He calmly asks for your driver's license and registration, goes back to his car, and then doles out a ticket as the consequence. Not a lot of chatter happens in this interaction, just stone-cold professionalism. This is the way that many consequences in the so-called real world are enforced. If we are trying to prepare our children for the real world, we should emulate such a model as best as possible.

CHILDREN WATCH WHAT YOU DO MUCH MORE THAN THEY LISTEN TO ANYTHING YOU SAY

Children mirror what they observe much more than anything they are told. Behavior begets behavior, and children are like little parrots of parental behavior. They are quick to ignore words, but they long remember actions.

This means that if you, as a parent, have trouble restraining your own anger, you should seek help. If, as a family, you find it challenging to solve problems without resorting to screaming, you should seek help. If you use profanity when you are angry, you should expect profanity when your children are angry. Remember, your kids are always watching and imitating you—both the positive and negative.

DON'T EXPECT TOO MUCH

Imagine that you are parenting a six-month-old infant and you are financially strapped because of the high cost of diapers and formula. You would be extremely motivated to potty train that baby, right? So why wouldn't you?

In short, common sense would tell you that it is an impossible uphill battle to toilet train an infant, because they are simply not developmentally ready. Their control over their infantile bodies and their developing intellect make the task all but inconceivable, and it would lead to anger and frustration to try.

This kind of frustration can occur at any level of a child's development. To avoid it, your expectations for what children can do must first be based on what is *possible* for them to do. This may seem like common sense, but let's look at an example of how this might play out with a five-year-old child:

Parent: "Go upstairs and get your shirt, pants, and socks on. Clean up your toys, brush your teeth, and come back down."

Child: "Okay." (Child goes upstairs.)

Ten Minutes Later . . .

Parent: "You have been upstairs now for almost ten minutes! What are you doing?"

Child: (No answer.)

Parent (going upstairs to find the child with a shirt and one sock on, quietly playing with toys): "What are you doing? I asked you to get dressed!"

How does this parallel the toilet training example? Consider the developmental abilities of a five-year-old. Most five-year-olds have an attention span of maybe five minutes on an assigned task. The extensive list that this parent required of this child is beyond what is possible for the child to retain. This too-high level of expectation leads to anger, resentment, and frustration for parent and child alike.

What if the parent tried to use a reward to get the child to do the same behavior—perhaps a toy car, a new video game, or time playing with a friend? It does not matter. Quite simply, if the child is not developmentally capable of a task, he or she is just not able to do it, no matter how motivating the reward. Consider the adult parallel: If you were offered a record deal for $20 million you might find it highly motivating, but if your singing sounds like a cat scratching a chalkboard it is nonetheless developmentally impossible.

Tables 2.1–2.4 illustrate some of the basics of child development. Please note that these are only a general reference, and all children grow and develop at their own unique pace. If you are concerned or unsure about your children's development, it is best to refer to your pediatrician, or another medical professional, for assistance.

Table 2.1.   Table 2.1 Infant/Toddler/Preschool

Emotional Development	Social Development Skills
Birth–1 Year: Learn the foundations of trust: Can I trust my caregivers to meet my needs?	Infant/Toddler: For attachment, infant looks for regularity and comfort from parents.
1–3 Years: Learn how to get the attention of those who care for them.	At 5 Months: Begin to read facial expressions and emotions.
12–18 Months: Know what they want but have difficulty voicing or showing it; frequent tantrums result.	At 9 Months: Begin to understand basic social interactions with others.
18–36 Months: Begin to comprehend the concept of "being good" or "being bad," and believe they are	At 11 Months: Become afraid of being away from parents or being around strangers.

Emotional Development	Social Development Skills
either "good boys/girls" or "bad boys/girls."	*At 2 Years:* Imitate those around them.
Develop knowledge to comprehend that those around them have feelings.	
Find toys or other objects necessary for security.	

Table 2.2. Preschool Age (36 months–5 years)

Emotional Development	Social Development Skills
Look to parents and others significant in their life as source of self-worth/-esteem.	Like to play, imagine, and interact.
Have an increased ability to control their feelings.	Continue to develop social skills.
Develop more patience and have fewer tantrums.	Begin to feel guilt when they do something "bad," and happiness when they do something "good" (in the eyes of their parents).
Start to understand that other people have needs versus being aware only of their own needs and wants.	Start to have an understanding and comparison of boy versus girl.
Begin to comprehend that there is a difference between right and wrong.	
Look to parents and other adults to support their self-confidence.	
Explore their world on their own and frequently ask, "Why?"	

Table 2.3. Elementary School Age (5–11 years)

Emotional Development	Social Development Skills
Self-esteem becomes based more on actions and how they are evaluated by parents, teachers, and coaches.	Friendships are no longer based on who is closest to the child in proximity; relationships develop centered primarily on shared interests.
Develop means to more effectively express emotions.	Understanding fairness and right versus wrong, and believing everyone should be treated equally.
Care about what other people think about them.	Rules and fairness are important in understanding the world: 5–6 Years: Rules can be changed to the child's advantage. 7–8 Years: Rules must be rigidly followed.

Emotional Development	Social Development Skills
	9–10 Years: Can discuss how to make rules fair for everyone in each situation.
	Pretend to take on different adult roles.
	Change behavior revolving around what they think they are supposed to do due to fit with their community.
	Can take on more responsibility at home.
	Prefer and understand team play.
	Begin to comprehend the basic concepts of ethics and morals.

Table 2.4.   Teenagers (12–19 years)

Emotional Development	Social Development Skills
Young Teens (12–14): Become self-conscious and worried about their body image; may take a negative view of their looks.	*Young Teens (12–14)*: Begin distancing themselves from their parents and moving more toward a peer group.
Become very sensitive to parents' criticism or being asked too many questions. May try risky behaviors in an effort to show independence from the rules of their parents. Become focused on peers and their opinion, and may not appear as concerned with parents' thoughts or spending time with their parents.	Being "popular" and/or accepted by peers is one of the more important aspects of their well-being.
Middle Teen Years (15–17): Compare and try to understand values and belief systems of other people Develop opinions, attitudes, and values that may be independent of those of their family.	*Middle Teen Years (15–17)*: Friendships become based on mutual understanding, loyalty, and trust Seek adults to treat them fairly and to be honest, open, and straightforward.
Start to establish a full self-image; struggle with finding out who they are and their actual identity.	Begin to note that morals and following the law are necessary for success in society and the larger world.

DISCIPLINE, DON'T PUNISH

Imagine for a minute that you, as a parent, are exhausted and in a foul mood. On top of this, your child is having a full-fledged temper tantrum. Do you:

1. Do nothing—you are too exhausted anyway; or
2. Scream and lecture your child; after all, doesn't he or she realize you are exhausted and you don't want to be pushed today?

If you punish your child, chances are good that you will opt to be more harsh as a reflection of your own sour mood, supported by the notion that your child has chosen to cross you on the wrong day and should somehow know better. Or, if the mood strikes you the other way, you might just fall asleep on the couch and opt to let exhaustion win out over action.

Now let's look at another similar scenario: You just got a raise at work, and you are well rested and in the sunniest of moods. Your child has that same temper tantrum. Do you:

1. Do nothing; you are in a good mood, so why generate all that negativity?
2. Give your child a harsh punishment and ruin an otherwise great day for both of you?

Chances are you will opt to "let him or her get away with it, just this one time." Why disrupt the feelings of happiness and bliss that you are riding upon?

This is the core concept of punishment: It is an action that is done without logic or consistency, instead depending on the random barometer of your emotions and energy. Therefore, the child learns that consequences are harsh, unpredictable, unsafe, or unfair—the perfect recipe for angry responses and more tantrums from the child.

The concept of punishment is often confused with the concept of discipline, but there is a difference between the two. When we think of professions, we often call them *disciplines*. This name is intentional because they require consistent, calm, and patient work toward learning the particular trade (or discipline). One can think of parental discipline as learning *the trade* of how to teach our next generation to handle emotions, negotiate conflict, and solve problems on their journey toward becoming adults.

Let's go back for a moment to the earlier example of the police officer pulling over a speeder. The officer should be disciplined in that they should treat you with respect regardless of how their own day is going or who you are. They should additionally provide you with the same consequence regardless of how tired they are: You were speeding by this much, so your ticket is this amount. The officer is to the point, unemotional, and consistent. The consequence is fair, logical, and undeviating. In return, you are expected to deal in a civil fashion with the world and laws of society (as well as those who apply them). When you don't pay a bill or are late, you pay a reciprocal penalty. No one is angered; it is just the consequence of the neglect to your real-world responsibilities.

Table 2.5 gives a brief overview of the comparisons and contrasting features of punishment versus discipline.

Table 2.5. Punishment versus Discipline

Discipline	Punishment
Done without a lot of chatter and nagging	Done with a great deal of needless chatter and nagging
Consequences are provided in a fair and relatively immediate fashion	Threats are either overly harsh or empty; consequences are inconsistent
Limits set are consistent, regardless of how the parent is feeling	Limits are harsher or nonexistent, depending on how the parent is feeling
Consequences make logical sense ("the punishment fits the crime")	Consequences are different each time and often don't make any sense to the child (i.e., "Because you did not eat your dinner, you cannot go to the park.")
Teaches rules of how to logically get along in the world	Teaches children to listen to those in authority no matter what and not talk back
Failure to meet family, school, or community responsibilities in a timely fashion results in the need to pay the inconvenience back in some reciprocal manner	Sometimes inconvenience must be paid back and sometimes you get a "free pass," depending on the whim of the day and the parent's fleeting emotional state

WHEN PLAYING THE SLOTS OR PLAYING CARDS IN THE GAME OF PARENTING, YOU USUALLY LOSE

If you have ever been to a casino, you've probably noticed that they often have bright lights, high-end restaurants, and beautiful accommodations. This is not an accident. The frequent "financial donations" made by gamblers have paid for the palace that stands before you. The golden roads are paved with the empty pockets of many a hopeful gambler.

What does this have to do with children and anger? Well, let's first take a look at those flashing and ringing slot machines. Watch the gamblers who are sitting by those machines. They are endlessly pulling the one-armed bandit, hoping for a payout. Let's suppose a gambler puts in $2,000 worth of quarters in one day sitting at the machine. She wins a few paltry payouts of one or two hundred dollars every few hours, and she believes she is lucky because she has received some payout from the machine. In reality, she has lost several hundred dollars in total and is, in fact, decidedly unlucky in the pocketbook.

So why do people do it? They believe that if they continue to play, they will eventually get a jackpot that far exceeds the money that they invested. In reality, that rarely happens—but human behavior dictates that we are inclined to play harder, if not smarter. If we get some kind of reinforcement—even if it is not consistent—we keep working. Maybe it is the first, third, or twenty-fifth time, but eventually gamblers will get some kind of reward if they keep trying—and that keeps them trying.

The lesson that is taught by the slot machines can also be correlated with children's behavior. If children learn that their parents will give in and provide them what they want, they simply learn to work harder.

The thought process from the child's perspective goes something like this: "Last time, Mom and Dad gave in to my tantrum eventually. If I do that again, it may take five minutes or fifteen minutes, but I will get what I want." So when parents are inconsistent in their handling of parenting issues, they inadvertently teach their children to act out harder—to up the ante or keep trying—and eventually they will get a payout when the parent gives in.

Now, let's continue the gambling analogy and discuss playing cards. If you were playing poker, you would likely keep your cards close to your chest and maintain a poker face. In fact, both of these phrases were born of the fact that when playing cards, the idea is to prevent your opponent from knowing the cards you have. Revealing any emotion about your cards may compromise your ability to win the hand.

What can this possibly have to do with parenting? Well, parents often say, "I don't know how to do anything that works when my kids are angry, they *just don't seem to care* about anything!" When asked what this means specifically, parents often relate that no matter what they try, the children say that they "don't care," and so how do you deal with an individual who doesn't care?

Imagine, however, the angry child who has told his parent what he *does* care about. What would the parent do? Simple: restrict, ground, or take away the very things the child cares about most. Let's take the example of a seventeen-year-old who asks for the the keys to the car. He is imagining going to pick up his friends, going to the movies or to a party. Then his parent says, "I saw your grades. You cannot have the car tonight! You are grounded!" The teen's plans come to a screeching, sudden, devastating halt. He slams down the keys with a loud, metallic bang, and what is the first thing he says? *"I don't care!"*

Does he, in fact, care? Of course he does, but giving his parent the satisfaction of knowing that the consequence is going to get to him is more than his pride can take—not to mention that it will give the parent an effective idea to bank on as a future consequence. Keeping their cards close to their chest with an "I don't care" is simply a much more effective strategy for kids.

So, what is a parent to do? Try translating the "I don't care" statement. When you hear "I don't care," translate it to this:

I do care. This consequence is really effective and not the one I would choose because it impacts me greatly. Please know that I am really hoping you will choose another, less impactful one, so I am going to desperately keep my poker face and hold my cards close in hopes you will change your mind.

3

IT IS NO ONE'S FAULT

Lack of Responsibility and the Rise of Anger

Nothing will ever change while you point the finger of blame. Out of responsibility comes possibility.

—Lisa Villa Prosen

Maddie's mother knows something is wrong with Maddie. She is not sure, but she notices that her daughter has a sickeningly sweet smell of fruit combined with a hauntingly dank smell of nicotine. She notices her daughter often has her windows open, even as the cold chill of the winter air creeps in and leaves her room unbearably cold.

Maddie's mother puts on her detective hat and begins a diligent search on the web. The smell, the finding of a strange "flash drive–looking" device, and discarded plastic veils that look like used car fuses that litter Maddie's room . . . what could it be? What do these clues have in common? Her mother puts together the evidence with the tenacity of a forensic examiner and realizes that her daughter has been vaping—inhaling nicotine using e-cigarettes.

After sitting quietly and pondering what to do next, she finally gets up the nerve later that day to confront her daughter. "Are you vaping?" she asks in a wavering tone that belies her uncertainty that she has the right to ask and even suggests a modicum of fear. Maddie instantly snaps back, "It is not mine! Why do you always blame me?" The conversation is abruptly ended with the slam of Maddie's bedroom door.

WHY A CHAPTER FOCUSING ON RESPONSIBILITY?

One of the greatest issues our children face today is a chronic inability to understand and accept responsibility. Grades, chores, discipline, mistakes—everything is always someone else's fault: parents, teachers, or peers. Children come to believe they bear no influence or responsibility over these issues.

Worse yet, as role models to the next generation, we as a society have neglected to demonstrate a good example of how to accept responsibility. Politicians, athletes, and all manners of esteemed professionals are among those who have demonstrated incredible lapses in judgment followed by lack of responsibility for those indiscretions.

WHAT IS THE CONNECTION BETWEEN ANGER AND THE LACK OF RESPONSIBILITY?

Blaming others is a favorite defense mechanism of children to avoid taking responsibility for their own actions. Why? Quite simply, it keeps them from having to be introspective and look critically at their own behavior and actions. It is a defense mechanism that is utilized so quickly and so often that some children (and many adults) do not initially know they are doing it.

When children take responsibility for negative behaviors, they have to accept that they have not lived up to their own expectations, or those of others, and they have to take a hard look at disappointment and guilt. It is easier to turn that energy around, deflecting it toward something or someone else. The payoff is that the child (or adult) feels marginally better, at least in the short term. The difficulty is that without taking control and looking at the problem, the child never learns or grows from the issue at hand.

SO WHAT IS THE BIG DEAL?

We all know adults who blame the world for their lot in life. They are the ones who are perpetually wronged, always have bad luck, and never had a break go their way. They blame everyone: the government, their parents, their job, their spouse. In the end, however, they end up miserable, a product of the self-imposed prison they cannot find their way out of. If nothing is ever their fault, it is never within their power to make a positive change.

How does this have such a detrimental impact on children and addressing their emotional outbursts?

- *If children look toward others to take responsibility for controlling their behavior, they never believe they can control their own behavior.* When children say, "You made me angry" or "You made me do it," what they are really saying is, "I have no control over my emotions. You are the one who controls me." This diminishes their ability to believe that they can independently grow and learn.
- *Blaming other people can add to children's anger toward themselves.* Depression is often described as "anger turned inward." Children who embrace the belief that everything is someone else's fault become hopeless to change anything and may turn that feeling onto themselves.
- *Blaming other people prevents development of problem-solving and conflict resolution skills.* Children who think or who try to convince themselves that everything is the fault of other people or external circumstances never attempt to solve issues independently. This means they will never try to find a better way to rectify conflict or problems and will turn to blame and anger as their sole means of handling issues.
- *Blaming other people can lead to blaming others as groups.* When children do not take responsibility for their actions, the people they blame become nameless and faceless enemies to their own well-being. Ultimately, this can lead to children stereotyping or blaming groups of people for their own frustration or lack of success.

TEACHING CHILDREN RESPONSIBILITY

When we fail to teach responsibility, our children become angry because the means of controlling themselves is always just outside of their grasp of control and influence. What they do, what their circumstances are—all of this is out of their control. It is no wonder they become helpless, bitter, and angry. Without the recognition that *they* steer their emotions and choices, they feel powerless in a world that does not orbit around their lives. They are ships that are totally at the mercy of the currents of life.

Parents often forget that we are teaching children how to grow into adults. Yet they are not adults, and because of this, they are not ready to occupy the role of adulthood; they need to grow into the world of adult roles and responsibilities. Perhaps as a result, we have the relatively new phenomenon of boomerang children who never leave the comfort of the nest of home.

For example, take the case of a child who is reported to misbehave at school. As parents, our first instinct may be to defend our child. When we defend her, however, we run the risk of taking away her responsibility for the consequences of her actions. It is that very understanding of a consequence, a cause and effect, that is a necessary life lesson. When we shelter our children from this understanding of how to handle consequences in an appropriate manner, they do not learn how to build a tolerance for handling anger or frustration in their own lives.

How did you learn your lessons in life? It likely was not from the parental "I told you so" that is the stuff of jokes and metaphors. It was from experiences, often the most difficult ones, that you learned how to navigate life's twists and turns.

During the preschool and early elementary ages, children believe the world revolves around them. This is why you often hear that we must constantly reassure children that adult behaviors (like divorce) are not their fault. Young children consistently look for how they have caused or created an issue, despite the fact that they may have little or no impact on its actual creation.

As youngsters get older and mature, they develop a more balanced belief in their abilities and their place in the larger world. Children recognize that they are not responsible for everything that happens, nor are they always the center of the universe. That being said, they do learn from cause and effect that they are responsible for what they do—unless, of course, we shield them from the consequences of their actions. Then they never truly realize the effect—positive or negative—that they have on those around them and on society in general.

In fact, this type of sheltering actually stunts a child's emotional growth. They are left to believe either that they are responsible for nothing (in which case, why bother?) or that they are responsible for everything (which can be too much to handle, which is overwhelming). Children must know what they are responsible for, as this is a key that allows them to take control of their lives as well as their emotions. Ultimately, their anger and emotional state is for them to resolve.

This is supported by psychology professor Jean Twenge, who examines Generation Y in her book *Generation Me: Why Today's Young Americans Are More Confident, Assertive, Entitled—And More Miserable Than Ever Before.* "To facilitate change," Twenge notes, "our youth must first realize and embrace mistakes. Only then can they develop an alternative strategy for how they will handle future scenarios."[1] Further paralleling this data are the increasing numbers of adult children have difficulty leaving their childhood residence. In fact, "in 2014, 20% of young adults were still living with their parents, a number twice the amount of the generation before."[2]

Every family, based on society and culture, has slightly different strategies for teaching children how to assume age-appropriate responsibilities. Nevertheless, like any skill or discipline, there are certain ground rules that should be considered, as illustrated in box 3.1.

Box 3.1: Ten Ground Rules of Teaching Responsibility

1. *Never do for children what they are capable of doing for themselves.* Doing tasks for children limits their belief in their own abilities and self-esteem.

2. *If you are mean to other children, those children will likely not want to be your friend.* Trying to repair relationships for children teaches them that they do not have to develop, maintain, and/or preserve their own friendships/relationships.

3. *If you steal or lie, you must make amends to the person (or persons) you harmed, and it will be uncomfortable.* Stepping in or not having children confront their actions prevents them from experiencing the discomfort that such actions should bring. Therefore, they do not learn to understand the nature of these consequences. Children must learn to apologize and make amends to those they have wronged, even if it is uncomfortable.

4. *If you procrastinate, you will have to make it up at some other time not to your liking.* When children do not do what they are supposed to do when they are supposed to do it, it will have to be made up—likely at some time inconvenient to their social life, technology time, or watching their favorite television shows. Not allowing children to learn that they must balance their

---

time prevents them from recognizing time management as an important and necessary skill; thus, their failure to do something becomes someone else's problem.

5. *If you spend it all, you will not have it when you want something bigger.* Purchasing items because you feel bad that your children have spent all their money does not teach them financial management or any concept of money. Learning the language of money means understanding what it is like to have to save or to not have money for something they want because they spent it elsewhere. This teaches that money and finances are finite.

6. *If you break it or mess it up, you must fix it or clean it.* Stepping in to fix broken items or clean messes only teaches children a lack of respect for material possessions.

7. *Treating others the way you want to be treated is important, as is teaching others the way you want to be treated by them.* The Golden Rule is the foundation of empathy. As parents, we must ask, "how do you feel when this happens you you?" Additionally, the natural consequence of not treating (or treating) others this way will become the reflection of how the child is ultimately treated.

8. *No one else can resolve your anger or determine your happiness but you.* Constantly trying to solve the mystery of what is bothering children or determining what they need to be happy only teaches them that their happiness and solutions to their anger must be found by someone else. Children must learn to determine (together with a parent or caregiver if need be) what they need to reach this goal.

9. *You are not going to succeed at everything; however, you are responsible for trying your best and determining what is "good enough."* Competition is about taking responsibility for your "personal best" versus trying to simply beat someone else or sulking over losing. This means that parents should help the child give an honest and balanced assessment of what they did right and what actions they can improve upon.

10. *Respect others.* Children who expect respect must be willing to give respect to others. This does not mean they should bend to whatever anyone tells them to do, but it does mean that they are responsible for treating others with a level of respect. It also means understanding that there is a structural order that exists between adults and children. Children must learn that in all organizations (formal and informal) there is a natural chain of command. This translates into how they may say their opinion respectfully, however, it does not mean that they may get their way in larger family, educational, or recreational activities/decisions.

ACCEPTING MISTAKES ALLOWS RESPONSIBILITY

When parents or teachers raise their voice to children, or harp on them for making a mistake, children learn to hide their errors and avoid taking responsibility. If adults instead confront mistakes of childhood directly, without judgment, anger, or belaboring the issue, children feel safe coming forward and taking responsibility for the small issues (and hopefully some of the larger ones). Remember that minute issues become big issues later with age, so teaching them to take responsibility for small issues now will set the foundation for open dialogue with the bigger issues later.

PROVIDE HELP, PROVIDE QUESTIONS, DON'T ALWAYS PROVIDE ANSWERS

The easiest and quickest way to assist children is often to do something for them directly or to simply provide the answer to a problem regarding homework or a social dilemma. This, however, precludes the opportunity to teach children how to take responsibility for themselves and develop problem-solving skills as well as wisdom.

Instead of solving a problem and taking the quickest way out (for both you and the child), ask questions that lead to independent processing and solution of the problem. Remember that the goal is not to just guide children with yes or no answers, it is to challenge them to think as well as to take responsibility for their problem-solving skills. This means asking open-ended questions.

Younger children especially can become easily confused between asking questions and making statements. In other words, when they ask you "a question," they tend to phrase it in terms of a statement or story. Therefore, be certain to model open-ended questions that begin with the words *who, what, when, why,* and *how.* These introductory words will be certain to generate dialogue rather than simple yes or no replies.

Some examples of open-ended problem-solving questions include:

- What do you think is the better choice?
- What will happen?
- How did you think of the consequences of both choices?
- What are the positives and negatives of either of the choices?
- How did you solve this type of problem in the past?
- How do you think I would solve this problem?
- How would you feel if this was done to you?
- What happens if you give up this sport/club/game/job? How would your teammates feel?

MAKE CERTAIN RESPONSIBILITY IS
TAUGHT AT HOME

In a society, each of us has a role. Our paid work is an example of this: Each of us does something that is of benefit to society at large, and so we are rewarded for it. Conversely, if we do not do anything of benefit to society, our reward is exponentially less.

Is this the case in your home? If you are teaching your children that they have no responsibilities, aren't you providing them an all-inclusive vacation, with free food, free cable television, and someone to serve at their beck and call? Most people pay good money for these services, but if your children get them for free, what is the reason to change anything?

If your children are accustomed to the all-inclusive vacation lifestyle, when you do try to change this situation, you will be faced with angry, irritable children who want things to go back to the status quo. Instead, let your children know that with benefits come responsibilities, with take there is give, and with choices there are consequences. (See box 3.2.)

Box 3.2: Sample Chore Charts and Age-Appropriate Responsibilities
Ages 4–5
- Help set the table and bring dishes to sink
- Assist in putting away non-glass/fragile groceries
- Make their bed according to their best ability
- Get dressed (with minimal assistance)
- Put clothes in hamper and/or sort clothes according to light and dark
- Organize books and toys in their room
- Help take care of pets

Ages 6–8
- Assist in vacuuming
- Take out lighter trash from rooms
- Help put away and fold laundry
- Brush their own teeth/comb their own hair
- Put dishes in and take dishes out of dishwasher

Ages 9–12
- Prepare lunches
- Help clean bathrooms
- Assist with the washer/dryer
- Keep bedroom clean independently
- Wake themselves and get ready for school (with the help of alarm clock)

Ages 13–18
- Do their own laundry

- Prepare meals
- Add what they need/want to the grocery list
- Discard old items in the refrigerator
- Do chores without being told
- Get a job to earn spending money
- Purchase items using their own money
- Be responsible for all aspects of their room, hygiene, personal items, and schoolwork

4

THE REVOLUTION OF CONFLICT RESOLUTION

Peace is not absence of conflict, it is the ability to handle conflict by peaceful means.

—Ronald Reagan

Joseph is a ten-year-old who, his teachers and parents have noticed, has difficulty getting along with his peers. Often, Joseph will either tell his peers off in a barrage of profanity, or bully others into giving him his way. Sometimes he will just simply cry, tantrum, and stomp his way out of solving a problem.

Many times, the issues Joseph encounters with his fellow classmates are seemingly minor issues. Yet each time he has a small challenge, it seems to blow up into a major crisis that causes him to get himself into trouble that often seems unwarranted.

His teachers and parents label Joseph as a child who "just can't seem to get along with anyone." Joseph often spends recess playing alone, as he has chosen to isolate himself to avoid potential difficulties with his classmates.

THE MYTH THAT ANGER IS A BAD EMOTION

If you ask most young children if they are allowed to be angry, they answer with a resounding "No!" Most children associate anger with rage and acting destructively. It is, therefore, a "bad" feeling that should be avoided at almost all costs.

Yet anger is an emotion that all of us feel, and it often helps with solving problems and setting boundaries; ultimately, it is useful in our personal development. Rage, on the other hand, is a destructive emotion that leads to explosion followed by implosion and can destroy relationships. These two states of feeling generally create confusion among most children, who then see anger as a shameful feeling that must be hidden because of its potentially damaging qualities.

Unfortunately, holding anger in creates feelings of depression or, when it is turned outward, generates the same consequence as shaking a bottle of a carbonated beverage and then opening it: the deluge explodes all over those around you. It is far better for anger to be leaked out slowly and in control than swallowed or held in and eventually spouted out.

Therefore, it is crucial that adults and educators teach children to harness anger and not to see anger as a bad emotion in itself but rather as an energy that needs to be appropriately channeled as a vital teaching tool and a useful quality.

TEACHING BOUNDARIES

If we are going to teach problem solving, we must also teach boundaries. Children must know where their physical and emotional limits begin and end, as well as how to protect and preserve these in a viable fashion:

- *Physical Boundaries:* These boundaries are concrete and include ownership of one's body, personal space, and material things. Explaining to your children that their bodies belong only to themselves and nobody else helps them develop a sense of physical self and an understanding that nobody should attempt to infringe on this. If someone does, they should immediately assert themselves and tell adults they trust until they are assisted.
- *Emotional Boundaries:* These boundaries are more difficult to observe because they are neither concrete nor physical. Good emotional boundaries are ones that do not allow others to hurt a

child emotionally, including by teasing or bullying. It is more challenging for children to understand that they do not have to—and probably should not—share items that are important to them with those they do not know well. This boundary is generally developed through adult assistance as well as trial and error.

KIDS LEARN THE MOST ABOUT PROBLEM SOLVING FROM ADULTS

As adults, we handle a great number of problems, large and small, each day. Yet when we make chronic mistakes in our own conflicts with our families, coworkers, and relative strangers, our children see this and reflect it in their own behavior. So it is vital that children see us handling conflict in a way that is effective and respectful.

In other words:

- *No blaming:* If you tend to blame others for your emotions, situations, or responsibilities, don't be surprised when you see that behavior emulated by your children. Model responsibility for your behaviors and your reaction to others' behavior toward you.
- *No profanity:* If you use profanity in your conflicts with others, you should expect that your children will find that type of vocabulary acceptable in their own conflict resolution styles. This may seem obvious; however, sometimes we are not aware of how we speak as it becomes a matter of course and habit.
- *Learn to say no:* If you are someone who says yes to everything and becomes overwhelmed, putting your self-care on the back burner, your children will notice this. It is necessary to be able to say no when your own needs require it and to teach your children to set boundaries accordingly.
- *Don't overtalk and belabor:* If you constantly harp on a conflict and repeat yourself over and over, expect your children to tune you out. If you find yourself asking, "How many times do I have to tell you?" you might want to think about who the slow learner is in the problem or situation.
- *Teach diversity in your handling of problems:* If you tend to blame particular groups of people or show prejudice in how you

handle problems, expect similar behavior from your children. When we place labels or stereotypes on others, children will emulate the same.

TEACH CHILDREN TO FORGIVE AND FORGET

Throughout our lives, we frequently run into people who are just plain difficult to get along with. Whether they are our bosses, coworkers, parents, acquaintances, or former significant others, they seem always to draw the most negative and bitter energy from the core of our very souls. Of course, when we spend time away from them continuing to harbor anger and resentment about their behavior or actions, thus, we give them even more power, influence, and our precious time, allowing them to further control us even when we are not in their presence.

Children are no different. They will often obsess about those who have wronged them, and they keep a mental tally. But the more time they dwell on the anger and remain in their own heads about how they have been betrayed, the less time they have to develop the positive relationships that are right in front of them. Additionally, continuing to dwell on this negativity and hatred only creates a negative loop of even more anger.

The answer is to teach children the concept of forgiveness. This is not to say that we teach children to allow their peers to walk all over them and spit in their proverbial eye without reaction. Instead, it means helping them learn to discard the emotional baggage of those they feel have wronged them.

Sometimes children think that forgiveness means that they have to play or spend time with a peer they don't like or care for. It definitely should not; instead, it means the following:

- *Model forgiveness:* If you carry a grudge, your children will learn that carrying grudges and the weight of that anger are acceptable and useful means of dealing with conflicts. Teach your children that you can get along with their other parent, your boss, or your co-worker solely for the understanding of the larger picture of those things that you consider a priority outside of the realm of petty grudges.

- *Teach them how to apologize:* Many children learn to just say "sorry." Unfortunately, this becomes more of a knee-jerk reaction, where they say it because they think it is the right thing to say rather than the right thing to do. When teaching children to apologize, have them also explain what they should have done differently. Apologies then become a lesson versus an empty obligation.

- *When you can't say it, find another way to show it:* At times our children (much like adults) become so filled with anger that it stifles their ability to say the words they so desperately need to say. Teaching children to write or draw their feelings allows them to grapple with finding the words necessary to discover forgiveness in a more effective and creative manner.

- *Teach them to understand before reacting:* Often children's egocentric thought processes get in the way of forgiveness. For instance, they may believe that they have been purposefully wronged, when in truth, their peer just was being self-centered and simply did not think of their feelings in the equation of the situation. Teaching children to look for potential alternate reasons for a friend's behavior makes forgiveness easier because they can see there was no malice behind the peer's actions.

- *Teach them that relationships take two:* Think of a relationship as two hands shaping clay into a sculpture. Which is more responsible? Both have a (literal) hand in making the piece of art. Relationships are much the same. Children have a hand in making the relationship what it is (or is not). Encourage children to see what was *their* hand in the situation. This is not to say they are at fault; however, it is good to teach them to look at their level of responsibility in all their relationships. As noted in the book *The Age of Enlightenment II*, "Peace doesn't require two people. It requires only one, it has to be you."[1]

DON'T BE TOO QUICK IN CONFLICT RESOLUTION

The caution against stepping in too quickly also applies to teaching conflict resolution skills. When we see a verbal conflict between our children or with another child, we want to step in to end it and defend our child. But this does not teach children the skill of conflict resolution that is crucial for anger management. It is better to teach them these skills that are necessary components of anger resolution skills. Some of the concepts will be discussed later in this chapter.

LOOK FOR CREATIVE SOLUTIONS TO CONFLICT

Like any of us, when children are engaged in an angry conflict, they have a tendency to ratchet down firmly on their viewpoint. They seek to prove only that they are right rather than solving the problem in a manner that resolves the situation adequately for both parties. Unfortunately, insistence on being right usually leads to a downward spiral of unproductive arguing, frustration, and ill feelings for both children.

FOCUS ON WIN/WIN VERSUS RIGHT OR WRONG

Teach children to focus on win/win rather than anger-provoking win/lose or right/wrong scenarios:

- *Focus on the issue:* Teach children to focus on the problem rather than insulting or putting down the peer they are having the issue with.
- *Find solutions that neither child may have thought of:* Work on having both children brainstorm several creative solutions rather than sticking to the limitations that are brought on by anger and irritation. This also teaches creative problem-solving abilities.
- *Begin with the goal in mind:* Teach children to look for what they want in a solution and then work their way back through the situation in a manner that is acceptable to both children.
- *Teach children the definition of a deal:* Children often have a challenging time understanding the concept of a deal as a way for everyone to get some of what they want, just not all of what they want. Adults can inquire as to what they want. What are they willing to give up/share to get that?
- *Look at the good and bad:* Teach children to look at the positives and negatives of all the possible solutions and ideas; this helps them find a balanced solution.

- *Don't allow technology to get in the way:* When children have a conflict, they tend to hide behind the relative safety of texting, e-mailing, and other such modern forms of communication. Not only does this make interactions in conflict unclear, it can also fuel drama and anger. Adults should encourage complex problems, or those that are of an emotional nature, and they should be resolved face-to-face versus under the safe veil of anonymity that technology provides.

ASSERTIVENESS IS A BALANCE

All of us handle conflicts in a manner that exists along a spectrum, from being overly passive to being assertive and, finally, to the far extreme of red-hot aggression. Most children and adults think of anger as being at the far end of aggression, but passivity and assertiveness are also vital pieces of the puzzle that is anger. Let's look at the following figure for a range of behaviors and aggression:

PASSIVE	ASSERTIVE	AGGRESSIVE
Anger Turned Inward	Balanced	Anger Turned Outward
Receives Less Attention	Well-Adjusted	Receives Too Much Attention
Feel Helpless	Feel Helpful	Feel Hopeless
Trouble Making Friends	No Trouble With Friendships	Difficulty Keeping Friends
Talks Too Softly	Talks In Average Tone	Talks Too Loudly
Stays Away from Groups	Team Member	Wants to Control Groups
Always Feels Guilty	Feels Confident	Always Feels Left Out
Doesn't Consider Self	Consider Self/Others	Consider Self Only
Feels the Victim	Feels Good	Feels Angry
Avoids Eye Contact	Appropriate Eye Contact	Excessive Eye Contact
Always Agrees w/Peers	Compromises	Never Agrees/Backs Down
Seeks Lose/Win (They Lose)	Seeks Win/Win	Seeks Win/Lose (They Win)
Dishonest w/Feelings	Honest w/Feelings	Hurtful w/Feelings
Low Self-Esteem	Good Self-Esteem	Inflated Self-Esteem

THE "I" MESSAGE

Perhaps one of the key components of assertiveness is also one of the simplest. The "I" message is taught to adults and children alike in counseling and as a foundational hallmark for developing assertiveness. This message is key because it does not allow children to point proverbial fingers at others and encourages them to own the part of an argument that is their responsibility.

The format for an "I" message is:

- *"I feel"*: How the child feels, specifically (i.e., angry, tired, sad).
- *"Because"*: The specific issue (from the child's perspective) that is causing the particular feeling.
- *"So I need"*: What the child needs (as specifically as possible) to solve this issue.
- Putting it all together, an "I" message may sound like: "I feel angry because you took my book without asking. I need you to give it back to me and apologize."

TELLING VERSUS TATTLING

Children—especially young children—often have difficulty distinguishing telling from tattling. This creates anger between both the child, who is allegedly tattling, and the peers whom the child is telling or tattling on. Tattling undermines the framework for children to use conflict resolution skills, because they are constantly and continually deferring issues to adults. Concurrently, tattling does little to sharpen their skills in problem solving. Finally, tattling creates an obstacle to making friends—the child earns a reputation as someone who will get others in trouble without batting an eye.

The question, then, is: How do we teach children to distinguish when they should tell an authority figure and when the issue is a minor situation that they can likely handle on their own? The distinguishing characteristics of tattling versus telling are the risk of potential danger or harm to oneself or others, urgency, or an inability to handle an issue (despite numerous attempts) at the children's current problem-solving capability. For more about this, see table 4.1.

Table 4.1.   Distinguishing Factors for Handling Issues

Minor Issue (Child Should Handle Independently)	Major Issue (Child Should Defer to an Adult Immediately)
Cutting in line	Pushing a child down in line
Arguing over a toy or other item	Peer hitting another over a toy
Peer taking a small, insignificant item	Shoplifting or taking items in a manner that would be illegal
Peer making faces at another	Peer making threatening gestures to another
Peer doing something accidentally to another	Peer intentionally attempting to hurt or bully another
Peer being "bossy" to another	Peer daring another to do something potentially dangerous or harmful

TEACH PROBLEM-SOLVING SKILLS

It is not enough to teach children the difference between telling and tattling; children must be given practical opportunities to use their problem-solving skills to deal with minor issues. "I" messages are certainly an effective way for children to assert themselves in potential arguments. However, the more tools children have in their proverbial toolbox to address a potential issue, the better off they will be.

Teaching children the following problem-solving skills can be very useful:

- *Give yourself a timeout:* As Lawrence J. Peter once said, "Speak when angry, and you will make the best speech you'll ever regret."[2] Teach children that taking a break from a potential conflict until they can solve it in an effective manner is sometimes the best answer.
- *Ignorance is bliss*: The skill of ignoring is a challenging one to learn. Many children think they are ignoring another when they tell others that they are ignoring them—thus violating the very principle of ignoring. Instead, teach children to pretend that the other cannot be heard or seen, nor can their presence be felt.

- *Brainstorming:* Often children become stuck on a single manner of solving a problem. When it does not work, they try that same strategy only harder (as discussed in chapter 2). Teach children to come up with as many other potential solutions as possible and to think about what would happen if each was used.
- *Admit when you are wrong:* It is difficult for any of us to admit when we are wrong, but teaching our children to do this—and to admit what they are apologizing for—can be one of the greatest forms of problem solving. Praise your child when they admit they are wrong. Don't just accept a blanket apology, but what they would no next time and how they will fix their error.
- *Test the solution:* Have children try out potential solutions (if they seem valid) to see if they have come up with a good solution. This is similar to trying an experiment to see if a hypothesis works.

ALLOW OPPORTUNITIES FOR PROBLEM SOLVING

The only way for children to learn problem solving, and the incorporated practical social skills involved, is by trying them out in real time. This means that the more opportunities they have to practice conflict resolution, the better they should ultimately get at these complex behaviors.

So how do we find these opportunities? Some suggestions include:

- *Play dates:* Play dates with peers are generally unstructured events in which children must learn social as well as problem-solving skills in a practical manner. This is also a time when parents can be in earshot to guide or make suggestions when necessary. Play dates are not to be confused with organized activities such as sports, crafts, or martial arts that is just another form of structured learning.
- *Sibling issues:* Watch how children solve problems with their brothers and sisters. This is yet another venue to make suggestions and guide (rather than lead) conflict resolution. Productive sibling rivalry can be a good place to try out problem-solving skills in a protective setting before children attempt them in the larger real world.

- *Organized activities:* Involving children in organized sports and other activities that naturally involve problem solving helps them sharpen these abilities. This is not to be confused with unstructured play.

5

THE MATCH

What Fuels Anger in Children?

Reactions come from the mind, responses come from the heart.

—Joseph Meyering Sr.

Seven-year-old Sami is excited about the prospect of going to the store with her mother. She has in her head that she simply must have the newest doll that will make her family of dolls for her dollhouse complete.

On the way to the store, she thinks, "I cannot wait to have that doll. When we get home she will play together with my other dolls. They will be one big, happy family. They will go on an imaginary trip and . . . " These thoughts swirl around in her head as they make the all-too-familiar turns and stops on the way to the store.

Before she can finish her pondering, they have reached the store. She pops out of the car and patiently waits as her mother goes from aisle to aisle, picking up items for the week ahead. Sami becomes both giddy and nervous as they approach the toy aisle.

As her mother gets near the toys, Sami can no longer contain herself. She runs to the doll that is neatly packaged on the shelf. With shaking hands, she shoves the box at her mother and proclaims, "This is the one I want!" Sami giggles with excitement that her life will soon be complete in her imaginary universe.

The only problem is, she hasn't told her mother about the dialogue in her head, and her mother has no plans to get her a $35 toy today. Her *mother breaks the terrible news: "No toys today." Sami realizes that this means no reunion of her doll family, no completion of her imaginary world. The world she had envisioned is now incomplete and crushed. Sami begins to kick, cry, and scream. She is devastated, grieving, and hurting.*

To add insult to injury, her mother says, "Oh, you are not going to have one of those meltdown temper tantrums again, are you? If you do this here, you are not playing with your dolls when you get home!" Sami's real and imaginary worlds have merged, and now both are shattered.

ANGER IS AN ELUSIVE EMOTION

Anger is the fuel that has powered competition and set assertive boundaries for generation after generation. When channeled productively, anger can be the impetus for people to do some amazing things. As we noted earlier, children, however, often assert anger with rage and violent outbursts.

ANGER HAS DEEP ROOTS

Anger is indeed a very complex emotion. We sometimes simplify it in terms of the frustration and fury we observe in children, but its roots are generally much deeper than we realize. Anger never exists as its own singular feeling; rather, it is usually a unique combination of frustration, fear, confusion, sadness, grief, lack of confidence, and a host of other negative emotions that dwell at its core.

Most children, however, see this emotion from a singular and simplistic perspective when they are angry; they understand simply that they are *just angry*. They lack the understanding that myriad of other feelings are at the core and that anger is only the outward expression of those other feelings.

Without recognition of this premise, it is very difficult for children to control their anger. It is like trying to pick fast-growing weeds. If you do not get to the root, they often grow back at a ferocious pace and overwhelm your garden. Anger is tough to control because it is not just one thing to handle; it is a complicated cocktail of emotional knots.

Understanding anger means understanding the emotions that lie at its very root.

ANGER COMES FROM TWO PLACES

Imagine driving down the highway and being cut off by a driver who speeds past you at breakneck speed. If you are like many people, your response is likely to react with profanity and maybe even flip the other driver the bird. You may experience the kind of tunnel vision discussed in chapter 1, in which you can think of nothing but how that idiot almost killed you.

In this scenario, you are experiencing those all-too-familiar feelings associated with road rage. For a brief moment, your emotions seem to overwhelm your sensibilities and, in so doing, can turn an ordinarily level-headed person into a screaming, irrational lunatic. Some people have been known to do things wildly out of character when they are under the spell of road rage. But why is this?

It is obvious that in this situation, our brain is seeking to fight. We think to ourselves that this uncaring driver has put the lives of others in peril and has no empathy or caring. What may not be as obvious is the reaction our body is generating: As adrenaline rushes through our body, our heartbeat increases, pumping blood to our arms and legs—and away from our brains—in preparation for a fight. In response, our brains switch to autopilot and ride the emotional wave of an adrenaline rush.[1] In fact, even when we believe our brain is clear and calm, this physiological reaction can still linger for quite a while after the initial crisis has passed.

How does this physiological response impact children's anger? Children—especially those who are younger—are often aware of what their brains are saying (i.e., "you're mad"), but they are unaware of the impact of the body's continued physiological reaction to this anger. In other words, they do not know that they are experiencing a continued fight-or-flight response.

Let's look at this another way: Imagine for a moment that you are boiling a pot of water. If you take the pot off the stove, what happens?

The water stops boiling almost immediately. However, what if you put that same pot back on the hot stove? The pot of water will begin rolling to a boiling again in no time. Why? Because the water never had the opportunity to settle back to anywhere near room temperature.

The physiological response to anger is much like that pot of water. When a child becomes angry, it triggers a fight-or-flight response in the body. The child begins ranting in response to the adrenaline pumping through his or her little veins. A well-intentioned adult may give the child a few minutes to cool off, but after that time the child is often set right back upon the metaphorical stove of whatever it is that triggered his or her anger. As a result, the child quickly returns to that boil of anger.

So what does this have to do with understanding how to handle a child in the throes of emotional turmoil? Well, it is important to learn to gauge when the child's thermostat has returned to room temperature.

As it turns out, Daniel Goleman, in his best-selling book *Emotional Intelligence*, points to an answer to this very question. His groundbreaking research determined that it takes "at least twenty [minutes] to clear your body of these emotions and arousal."[2] This provides a road map to help us understand how long it should be before we approach an angry child. Put another way, if that steam we addressed earlier is coming out of the ears, wait twenty minutes before trying to put anything new into the brain.

THE BRAIN IS A SUPERCOMPUTER IN ANGER

At some point, many children become aware of what tends to trigger their anger. They may realize that if A occurs, they usually do B, and then C happens as a reaction from others. This understanding should make changing the behavior as easy as manipulating those variables.

The only problem is that children's brains are like efficient supercomputers. Once the brain realizes the ABCs of their anger, it is simply easier to go from A to C and skip the middle variables altogether. Sometimes children do not even know why they do what they do. This is why it is important that we slow down and reexamine the ABCs of their behaviors with them, to help them understand the why of the equation.

HOW ANGER IS FUELED

Think about how your own anger is fueled. Anger comes in waves: You think you have calmed down, then you remember something else that reignites the inferno. You mull over how unfair something was, how rude your coworker is, how uncaring your boss can be, or how someone did not reciprocate what you did for them. Whatever it is, as you remind yourself of these things, you pile more kindling on the burning flames of your anger.

Next, let's take a look at how children's thinking impacts their anger and sustains it for a longer period of time than may be necessary or warranted. These skewed ways of thinking about the world allow anger to carry on for needlessly prolonged periods of time. However, these vocational perceptions often become reality because children rarely question the thoughts that reverberate within their heads. Their thoughts become 100 percent reality and are typically not analyzed any further.

Life Is Unfair

As adults, we realize that life is unfair, or at least unequal, in a variety of ways. Some people are born with more advantages, and who you know may be a bigger factor than what you know in your job as success or failure. This is a frustration we all grapple with, and eventually most of us come to the unsettling conclusion that unfairness is simply an inevitable part of life.

Children, however, concretely equate *fairness* with *equality*, believing, for instance, "If you get something, I should too." This notion, of course, is ridiculous. After all, if my sister gets a brand-new pink dress, equality demands that I should get the very same thing, whether or not I want it. If I went to the doctor for a sore throat and a patient went in before me with a broken arm, equality would demand that we receive the same treatment. Children must be taught that *fair* means everyone gets what they need, not that they are treated in the exact same fashion. Fairness is fluid and changing, not concrete and inflexible.

An example of how this fans the flames of anger is when a child thinks:

No one is fair to me. Everyone gets more than I do. I have the right to be angry because everyone gets more or is treated better. If I don't show my anger, everyone will continue to get more than me and I will get less than others—or perhaps nothing at all.

No One Likes Me. . . . Life Is Always Negative

Have you ever looked at the air filter in your home? It has the most distasteful job of filtering out all the hair, dander, mold, and other pollutants from your home so that cleaner air can be dispersed through your heating ducts. But sometimes it becomes bogged down with too many contaminants, and then it blows the very things it is supposed to filter out into every part of the house.

Children—and adults—sometimes harbor a parallel manner of thinking: They fail to filter the positive in themselves and others. They have a unique ability to pull the negative out of any conversation or interaction and let the positive go in one ear and right out the other. Without any positives, they can then justify their anger with the belief that nothing works out for them and that they are always the victim of others or of plain bad luck. In this way, the pollutants of toxic thinking are left to circulate around every aspect of their lives.

An example of how this fans the flames of anger is when a child thinks:

> The world is always against me. Why bother even trying? Everything I do fails anyway. I can do nothing perfectly, so why try? If you push me to do something, I will not be capable of doing it to my level of perfection, so why even take a shot at it? It will just lead me to become frustrated and angry!

I Know Exactly What Is Going to Happen Next

In our fast-paced world, it is natural to try to predict what is going to happen next. We may try to guess what the future holds or attempt to read someone else's mind or behavior—a skill that most people are notoriously bad at.

Children in particular often believe that they know what a peer is going to do and then surmise a reason for it. Yet they do so with little or no supporting evidence and don't ask questions to confirm their hypothesis. They simply react with their emotions and without logic, believing that their intuition must be accurate. As mentioned earlier, children tend to be egocentric; this bolsters their belief that they must be correct in their assertions about others.

In many cases, children assume these behaviors are assumed to have a negative intent. For instance, a child who reads a text that is mostly neutral in content may assume that the sender is being sarcastic or obnoxious, even when that is not the intent. When they do this, children tend not to test whether what they are thinking is based in even a shred of truth; they just react and fly off the handle with emotion versus logic.

An example of how this fans the flames of anger is when a child thinks:

> How rude! Joey walked by me in the hallway and didn't even say hi. There was no reason he had to be that way to me! Maybe he's mad at me. You know what? How dare he be mad at me! Since he was nasty and ignored me this morning, I am going to be mean to him. I knew he was a jerk anyway and could not be trusted!

I FEEL IT, THEREFORE IT IS TRUE

As we come to find out in the wisdom of adulthood, our feelings are not logical; they just *are*. When we feel angry, we can talk ourselves off the ledge by recognizing that there is no logical basis for the feeling. Children tend to lack that understanding of feelings versus logic. Therefore, a child who feels that he or she is a bad kid believes he or she must be one, and a child who feels that someone doesn't like him or her believes that must be true. The issue is that these rigid snap judgments are often made with little or no accompanying evidence.

An example of how this fans the flames of anger is when a child thinks:

> I feel as though I did something that was bad, so that makes me a bad kid. If I feel I am mad, that means I can act out in an angry way. My feelings make me do it, because it is how I am feeling and who I am, and that entitles me and causes me to act this way.

LABELING PEOPLE INSTEAD OF JARS

It is human nature to label people. When we are driving on the highway of life, those who are driving faster than us are "those crazy maniacs," and those who are slower are "those stupid idiots." The question then becomes: What are we in the eyes of those other drivers? Chances are we good that are driving too fast or slow for others' liking, and they may be labeling us accordingly.

In our anger we often create labels that take away the perspective of seeing others as people. For instance, instead of seeing another child as a potential friend, a child who feels he or she has been wronged may apply the label of "jerk" (or worse). It is far easier to hate a jerk than an occasionally inconsiderate peer, friend, teacher, or authority figure. The label also allows the child to feel validated in treating another person negatively.

Thus, we have to encourage children who are angry to discuss what it is they are angry about and to think about what the other person is *doing* that they feel needs to be changed, rather than simply accepting that they are angry and offhandedly calling the other person a name (and label).

An example of how this fans the flames of anger is when a child thinks:

> That kid is a jerk! Since he is a jerk, he has no good qualities. There-fore, I have the right to be mean to him and hurt him. That other kid is a nerd! That makes him not as good as me, so I can bully and harass him!

Or (more behaviorally specific):

> Joey doesn't ever listen to me. He takes my things without asking, pushes me around, and never says anything nice to me. Sarah is always into talking about things I have no interest in and that I think those topics are not at all interesting or cool. We are nothing alike and have very little to talk about.

The Sky Is Falling

Anger and anxiety often go hand in hand. When we are frightened, we become more irritable and likely to have a knee-jerk reaction because we are more easily bothered and angered. If you have ever had someone sneak up on you and your first instinct was to slap him or her, then you understand this: You simply reacted to fear first rather than thinking about potential consequences and planning your action or reaction.

Now, when everything becomes a worrisome crisis of worst-case-scenario thinking ensues, a child's life goes into survival mode, and that child acts out of desperate anger and emotion. Additionally, children generally can recognize both anger and sadness but often don't realize when the two overlap and become frustration (a unique concoction of sadness and anger).

An example of how this fans the flames of anger is when a child thinks:

> I can't do this homework. I'll never be able to do it! I hate this homework. I hate school! I am going to fail, so why bother? I give up. . . . I can't do it. (This is generally followed by an angry temper tantrum.)

IT'S ALL ABOUT ME

Most young children think the sun rises and sets around them, but as they grow older, a natural part of their development is beginning to empathize with others and recognizing that they are not the only one who exists in the world. Yet most children never completely overcome that self-centered perspective in their youth. (In fact, some people don't seem to overcome it even well into adulthood.)

Because they are so self-centered, children tend to think that every situation *must* have something to do with them. This gives them the false sense that they are always being talked about or that the world revolves around them and their actions. When they see two peers whispering, they believe their peers must certainly be talking and snickering about them, when in fact most discussions in the world around them have very little—or nothing—to do with them at all. The child must ask themselves critically, "Does this have anything to do with me? If so, how?" If it does, only then should the youth determine how to react.

An example of how this fans the flames of anger is when a child thinks:

> Mary is playing with Sarah today. That must mean she does not want to play with me! She must not like me. Maybe she even hates me! I must have done something to make Mary mad at me. What is wrong with me? What is wrong with her?

MY WAY OR THE HIGHWAY

Children's thinking is generally very concrete at the outset: It must be this way or that way; it is either everything or nothing. This kind of thought process leads to anger because they are unable to see any of the gray areas of potential resolution that may exist in a particular situation. For instance: "I am right; you are wrong!" "We will do it this way only!" Or in the case of a child having a substitute (or new) teacher, "My teacher does it this way, which is the only right way!" In each of these cases, there is no discussion of the myriad potential alternative solutions.

Encouraging children to discuss alternate ways of handling a situation teaches problem-solving skills. There is their way, their peer's way, and, generally, a third, more compromising way. Encouraging children to make compromises in which everyone gets something they want teaches them a vital and necessary life skill. Learning that instead of an either/or solution, there can be a both/and solution that better meets everyone's needs is an infinitely useful life skill that fosters a degree of teamwork and mutual understanding.

An example of how this fans the flames of anger is when a child thinks:

> You are playing checkers the wrong way! This is *the* way to play checkers, and *I* make the rules! Your rules are *wrong*, and there is *no* other way to play! Either you play my way, or I quit!

A compromise might be:

That is how *you* play checkers, and *I* am used to playing it this way. We have learned different rules and different types of checkers games. Both of us can adjust the rules so the game is fair for both of us.

HOW TO PUT OUT THE SPARKS OF ANGER BEFORE THE INFERNO ARISES

Accentuate the Positives

Often when children become angry they will fan the flames with statements like "No one likes me," "They hate me," "I hate myself," and so on. This downward spiral of negativity, low self-esteem, and desperate anger creates an inferno from a small spark.

The natural adult reaction is to try to rescue the child from this tailspin. Adults will often try to reassure children with comments like "Of course we love you" or "No one hates you, and here are the reasons why. . . ." What this does, however, is create a void that children can only fill with adult support. But what if the adult is not there?

Of further concern is that if children need others to provide verbal praise when they are sad, uncertain, or feeling sorry for themselves, they grow into adults who have to rely on others, clingy relationships, or even substances to fill the constant void of uncertainty.

A far more effective strategy is to encourage children to seek out positive things about themselves or their situation: "Tell me three positive things about you. Tell me three good things that are going on." By doing this, adults encourage independence and effective skills that children can use to pull themselves out of an emotional rut that will otherwise lead only to further anger, frustration, and, eventually, learned helplessness.

Ask: What Is the Worst Thing That Can Possibly Happen?

If you are a worrier, you are accustomed to the constant drumming of "what if" thinking in your head. Listening to these incessant ruminations can drive children to the brink of fear, irritability, or anger. It is akin to the man tucked behind the curtain in *The Wizard of Oz*: The thoughts become enormous, blowing flames of despair that look larger and scarier than they truly are.

However, when children are able to voice, draw, play out, or write their specific concerns or worries, they become smaller and smaller. When children are encouraged to talk through "the worst thing(s) that can possibly happen," many of these scenarios suddenly lose much of their grip over their thoughts. Further, when you encourage children to state how each of these worst-case scenarios could be handled, the thoughts lose even more of their grip on one's emotions. These children begin to realize that they (or the adults around them) can help them control most of those worst-case scenarios in a manner that will not cause their world to collapse around them.

Set Aside a Worry Time

Worrying in itself can be useful in developing proactive coping skills to handle particular issues or concerns. It is when these thoughts infringe upon a child's social, academic, behavioral, or mental health that they become of major concern. Put another way, worrying and anxiety are not problematic if they are put in their place and not given free rein to wreak havoc in the minds of our children.

Hence, worrying should be relegated to a period of time (say, fifteen minutes a night) when the child can pour out all of his or her worries in this designated time and space. Worrying should be done and shared only in this timeframe. Why? The child is disciplining his or her mind to make a time and place for everything—including worry and anxiety.

Scaling

As noted earlier, if everything is an emergency, then nothing is an emergency. If everything is a crisis, then nothing is a crisis. Children who live in a world of constant chaos do not develop the ability to prioritize concerns and learn to put every issue on equal footing. This creates a distorted way of thinking about what is a problem and limits their ability to make rational choices accordingly.

Additionally, when children believe that everything is an emergent crisis, this gives them permission to respond with a knee-jerk reaction of irritability or anger. If we encourage them to instead scale items—1 being the best and 10 being the worst, for instance—we create a means for prioritizing issues in a manner that is more sensible. It suddenly becomes clear that every situation does not involve either utter calm or outright rage and anxiety. The more frequent middle ground suddenly makes sense, and the majority of life situations and problems become more manageable.

The Goods and the Bads

When children feel angry, helpless, or sad, they often develop intellectual arguments to prove that they are right. (Many of these are discussed in the scenarios in the previous sections.) The problem is that when you are angry, you have no true balance of thought. Everything tips on the emotional scale of *terrible, unfair, my friends are against me, the world is against me*, and other such distorted means of thinking.

Is it any wonder why children become increasingly angry? They see no alternatives aside from the most radical responses. Having them write out the "goods and bads"—the positive and negative aspects—of each situation helps them develop a more balanced and rational approach to problem-solving. This is also a foundational step toward critical and productive thinking.

The Best Friend Method

Children often turn anger inward and use it to fuel their own frustration, whipping themselves into an emotional frenzy. They become their own worst enemy, based upon what they tell themselves in reference to a particular situation. They tear down their own self-esteem and, in turn, create an infinite cycle that can swiftly become a lifelong routine of negative thinking patterns and spiraling self-confidence.

Children do not generally question these harsh critiques of themselves. After all, as discussed above, whatever they are thinking must certainly be true because they have thought it. A more balanced cognitive approach can be to ask a child, "Would you say that to your best friend? If it is unacceptable for you to make those statements to your closest friend, then it is not okay to say it to the most necessary person in your life: *you*."

An example of this strategy might look like this:

Child: "I have no friends. No one likes me! I am stupid and can't do anything right!"

Adult: "Would you say that to your best friend?"

Child: "No! They would not like that or be my friend then."

Adult: "What would you say to your best friend?"

Child (thinks for a moment): "You have Joe, Michael, Sarah, and Tim as your friends, so what you are saying is not true. You are liked by a lot of people."

Grief and Loss

Grief is a complex emotion that comes in waves, ebbing and flowing like an ocean tide. Just when you think you are healing, it pulls you again into its undertow. When you combine this with children's generally short attention spans, they are constantly falling in and out of thoughts of grief and the complex emotions that drag behind it.

Since grief is such a challenging emotion for children to wrap their heads around, adults should expect that they will show feelings at unpredictable times as they grapple with a traumatic situation. Thoughts of loss, grief, and anger may occur as they think about the situation and then quickly leave as they move on to another thought. They may just as suddenly return to the subject of grief as something else sparks a memory of the loss.

When we see anger related to grief or loss, it is important that we reach beneath the surface anger to the true feelings of sadness, fear, anxiety, and lack of control; for example:

Child: "I am mad at you, I want my dad back!" (Child begins to have a tantrum and throw items.)

Parent: "You seem sad that you miss your dad."

Child: "I am not sad. I am very mad!"

Parent: "Maybe you are mad and sad because you miss him so much."

Child: "I do miss him, and I want him to live with us again." (Child begins to cry.)

Reaching beneath the surface anger in this case allows the parent and child to have a productive dialogue regarding the child's feelings of grief and loss.

Don't Allow Them to Think Tears Are Not Okay with Grief

As adults, in times of grief or loss we often try to hide these emotions from our children. The misguided belief is that if we cry, we will scare our children or let them know that something is not okay. In turn, we may believe we have to be strong for our children.

The problem is that when we try to hide our feelings from our children, they learn that certain emotions are not acceptable to display. For instance, if a parent does not cry at a sad situation, the child may believe that his or her crying will make the parent upset. Instead, the child allows these emotions to build up and sometimes erupt as anger and rage.

Emotions in times of grief or loss are part of the healing process, and a range of feelings can be expected. Children are watching to learn what behaviors are acceptable and unacceptable to be displayed. They often are fearful that their own strong emotions will somehow cause or add to a parent's own turmoil.

6

A KINDER, GENTLER SCHOOL

How Anger Can Be Handled in Schools

The highest form of wisdom is kindness.

—The Talmud

Luis is a fourteen-year-old Hispanic male student who has enrolled at a new school. He only recently emigrated from his native country of Mexico and is still struggling to learn the language and customs of his new home country. He is homesick for his friends and the family he left behind in his homeland.

His newfound peers tease him about his accent and tell him to "go back to where you came from." They are careful to do it out of the earshot of teachers so as not to get in trouble. Luis wants desperately to ask the teachers for assistance with this, as it weighs heavily on his heart and mind; however, his peers tell him he will be "a snitch" if he does so. Luis, who is still trying to make friends, decides against it, and buries the anger deep inside.

When Luis goes home he does not have a computer or any other technology to keep in touch with the few peers he would consider to be potential friends. It seems that everyone else has computers or smartphones, and they are constantly talking, texting, or otherwise chatting on social media.

Luis decides to go to the library to get on the internet, where he finds mean and hurtful rumors about his family posted by several of his peers on social media, including comments that he should "go back home" and that he "is not welcome in their school." Luis crumples in a heap, crying softly in his hands. He wonders aloud, "Why are my classmates so very mean?"

ANGER IN SCHOOLS

It seems that every week we hear of another terrible tragedy of school brutality occurring somewhere in the United States. The scenarios are slightly different, but the end result is always the same: innocent youth hurt or killed at the hands of barbaric anger and hostility.

Violence in schools is on the rise, according to David and Roger Johnson, authors of *Reducing School Violence through Conflict Resolution.* In their research they found that violence among children is definitely increasing: "From 1982 to 1992, juvenile arrests for homicides increased 228 percent; the homicide rate among teenage males (15–19 years) more than doubled between 1985 and 1991."[1] Paralleling this statistic, workplace violence among adults has escalated as a correlating indication of a society that is turning toward violence in ever-increasing numbers.

ARE WE LOOKING IN THE RIGHT PLACES FOR ANGER?

It is often easy to pick out children with a behavioral issue in school: They are the ones flipping over desks, cursing out the teacher, or refusing to follow the directions of any authority figure.

These are the children who get the services: They are given school counseling, are assisted by teacher's aides and paraprofessionals, and are the subject of numerous parental and faculty meetings to figure out ways to address the problems they present in the educational environment. These children have a way of grabbing every faculty member's attention and generally have numerous adults at their beck and call based upon their misbehavior.

Yet these may not always be the students who necessarily need the majority of our attention. What about the ones who turn their anger inward? The ones whose rage and torment lie dormant for an extended period of time? The ones who keep it bottled up, with rage boiling just under the surface, like a volcano waiting to be awoken?

If we are going to work with children who are exhibiting maladaptive behaviors, we must look at both sides: those who exhibit aggressive behaviors as well as those who show depressive behaviors and do not have an outlet for positive interactions. It is those who have no social outlets who increasingly turn inward, becoming despondent and letting their anger simmer inside their minds and bodies.

Unfortunately, the latter do not generally make themselves known to school personnel. They remain perpetually under the radar and need to be readily drawn out. They tend to stand out most in the places where adult supervision is minimal. Recess, lunch, physical education class, and hallways that tend to have minimal adult presence, where children's interactional inabilities or habits tend to be more tangible in these environments. These children may also show their true feelings on social media or blogs.

PRAISING INTROVERSION

It is important to understand that we are not necessarily talking about students who are introverted. Introversion does not mean that something is inherently wrong with a student or that he or she is harboring some deep-seated anger. As a society, we tend to praise more extroverted qualities, whereas many other cultures recognize the positive attributes those who are more introverted bring to the table.

There are many benefits of being introverted that should be recognized and celebrated in educational environments. For instance, those who are introverted often develop deeper, higher-quality relationships; they also tend to be more empathic. They are also careful about what they say and how they say it, so they generally understand interpersonal interactions better than extroverts do.

We cannot, and must not, confuse inward-focused anger or maladjustment with introversion. Children who are introverted enjoy the solitude found in being alone as well as in self-reflection, finding a sense of peace in these ventures. Those who are quietly angry, however, are using a distorted and rageful mirror to look at their own negative qualities—or those of others—but they do not have anyone to help them change that distorted reflection. We must look at mental health globally for all children, not just the one's who disrupt or go against the grain of a school's routine.

NOT EVERY KID IS A SCHOLAR, NOT EVERY KID IS AN ATHLETE

As adults, we all have different hobbies: Some of us like sports, others like to read, some enjoy technology or a host of other idiosyncratic hobbies that potentially few others may be interested in. Students sometimes fall through the cracks because they don't want to be involved in the formal school activities that others generally enjoy. They are stuck in a purgatory of trying to fit in with peers and their corresponding interests.

Finding "a hook," that is, an interest or a passion, for what these students who don't seem to fit in with the interests of most other students is vital. It is important to develop and tailor interests and hobbies (i.e., technology, LEGOs, card games) that bind them with their peers can help them find a place to belong in the school culture. Starting clubs tailored to these varied interests can help students find their way in an educational domain they were previously distant from, resentful about, and potentially angry at. It is necessary for faculty to think outside the box to reach students who think outside the box.

DEVELOPING PRACTICAL SOCIAL SKILLS

There is a lot of talk about socioemotional learning in schools and about the blanket term *social skills*. These skills are developed using social skills games and other curricula that address concepts ranging from making friends to divorce to self-esteem. These modalities all have a very valuable place in the hands of skilled school counselors and educators.

We must be careful, however, to ensure that these tools do not take the place of learning the practical application of social skills. For instance, sometimes the school counselor or other mental health professional may counsel students individually to help them develop social skills. The problem is that these children are generally able to talk to adults about social skills, or any number of subjects, without reservation. In fact, interaction with adults tends to be their strong suit, and many prefer it over talking with other youth. It is that very peer-to-peer dialogue that these students struggle with greatly and choose to steer clear of.

If social skills are taught solely in the sterile atmosphere of the school counselor's office, students miss the most challenging and important aspect of socializing. Socialization is an ever-changing carousel that is dependent on the environment and the peers with whom one is speaking. In other words, the way I speak in a particular situation or with a specific acquaintance may be wholly different from how I speak with a close friend or a classmate; this is also dependent upon the situational factors that influence these interactions. Thus, students who do not develop flexibility in their conversational and social skills become lost in the rapidly changing context of the surrounding community environment.

Social skills, then, are perhaps best taught from a sort of life coach perspective. This occurs when counselors (or other designated faculty) are at those places in which children are the most free to be themselves and interact openly, honestly, and with unfettered dialogue. These are areas like the playground, the lunch room, the physical education class, and the like. Only when counselors or other professionals witness these interactions firsthand can they give practical coaching on social and conversational skills. These are the actual environments in which practical social skills can be voiced, practiced, and perfected with an ever-changing dynamic that they present.

SYSTEMIC CHARACTER EDUCATION

In public schools we often see a wide pendulum swing in ideas, curricula, and subject matter. We go from one new idea to another, then abruptly back to a former one that is dusted off, retried, and suddenly regarded as "new" again. Eventually, that complex pendulum rests somewhere near the middle for a short while before it eventually, restlessly moves yet again.

Some of these ideas are the proverbial one-trick ponies: those that have limited focus and look at a minute piece of a complex educational system and don't recognize the need to step back and view the system as a whole. What they fail to address is that schools are increasingly complicated, living systems with many students, faculty, departments, and levels of intricacy. When a program myopically meets only one aspect of the educational system, it fails to make the appreciable impact necessary and, as a result, will likely be forgotten before the bell of the next day of school.

Systemic change in character education must:

- Survey all stakeholders as well as to determine areas of character education and school climate needs before the implementation of any program. This should include looking at:

  - Incidents of bullying and other forms of violence
  - Disciplinary issues
  - Faculty attendance
  - Student attendance
  - Faculty and student views of school and morale
  - Suggestions and recommendations by all stakeholders

- Be inclusive of all students and grade levels.
- Include routines and traditions that regularly celebrate student and faculty character on a daily (or at least weekly) basis.
- Include frequent and notable reminders throughout the school environment and curriculum to ensure support of appropriate school character climate.
- Provide training to all stakeholders of the school community: administrators, teachers, students, parents, secretaries, cafeteria workers, bus drivers, and so on.
- Feature a planned-out curriculum that extends throughout the academic year and includes a vision for systemic change (versus change that is limited in scope).

CHARACTER EDUCATION IS NOT ENOUGH IN THE TECHNOLOGY AGE

Character education is certainly an important and vital element of any school's climate and curriculum. However, technology has created a parallel universe in which children now simultaneously exist in two worlds. The technological universe is not always what it seems, and it is a domain where others can hide under a veil of relative anonymity, and gives them the opportunity to take out their frustrations on hapless fellow students in the form of cyberbullying.

Because of this, the character education trait of citizenship may be part of an outdated paradigm, as it is not inclusive of everything it means to be a child in modern-day society. Rather, digital citizenship (how to interact and function in the digital community safely) must also be taught in tandem with the traditional trait of citizenship.

The universes of the internet and of flesh-and-blood society now intersect in so many ways that we must ensure that students are prepared for the overlap. In fact, it may be even *more* important that we prepare students for the world of the internet, now and in the foreseeable future, then in many other social arenas.

TARGETING THE BULLY IS SIMPLY NOT ENOUGH

In recent years—and for good reason—focus has been placed on dealing with bullying, intimidation, and harassment within schools. This has been due to the horrible impact of bullying, which has prompted students to engage in emotional or physical harm to themselves and sometimes others.

That being said, for bullying to truly take hold and spread, it must have an environment that allows it to optimally exist. This means that more than just the bullies, and more than just their targets, are part of this equation. It means that those peers around them who do nothing—or, worse yet, encourage these behaviors—must be brought into the fold of potential answers.

An internet search reveals countless videos that students have recorded of their peers fighting and being bullied with the full encouragement of a crowd. These distorted viral videos, which provide a sensational perspective of children's inhumanity toward other children, are viewed over and over. They are popularized as a warped version of entertainment for some of our next generation, and some even make the national news.

It would seem to be human nature to stand up for others who are being bullied, harassed, or intimidated, and it is something children should naturally embrace. Unfortunately, that is not always the case. Studies show that most people—children and adults alike—will wait for someone else to do something because they are afraid to be the first to get involved in an emergent or hostile situation. Children, facing peer pressure and often being awkward socially, are not likely to do much better in these types of situations than their adult counterparts.

A case in point is that of Kitty Genovese. At around 2:30 a.m. on March 13, 1964, the young woman was returning home from her job as the manager of a bar in New York City. She was brutally attacked for well over half an hour as she screamed and pleaded vigorously for her life. The horrid screams pierced the quiet night air and were heard by thirty-seven of her neighbors, all of whom admitted to having been awakened by her cries. Yet no one did anything; no one called the police or took the few steps that might have changed her awful fate.[2]

When those who had heard the cries of Kitty Genovese were asked why they did not do anything, most of them indicated that they simply thought someone else would act first. Others indicated they did not want to get involved, and still others claimed to not recognize the severity of what was going on. This became the basis of what is now commonly known as the bystander effect. According to *Psychology Today*, this phenomenon can be defined as *"perceived diffusion of responsibility* (onlookers are less likely to intervene if there are other witnesses who they believe are more likely to do so) and social influence (individuals monitoring the behavior of those around them to determine how to potentially act)."[3] In other words, peer pressure indicated that someone else would do it, so everyone waited in a type of peer paralysis.

CREATING UPSTANDERS VERSUS KEEPING BYSTANDERS

How do we circumvent the bystander effect with our children? Let's take a look at another, parallel example: In medical emergencies, it has been found that people are much more likely to render aid to those who need it if they have been taught the basics of what to do.[4] So education about what to do, and how and when to do it, is the key to empowering individuals—students and parents alike—when an emergent crisis arises. Thus, we must teach students not to wait for someone else to act in cases of bullying, and we must educate them on what to do proactively.

The term *upstander* has become fashionable in the vocabulary of educational systems. As the term suggests, it requires a more active role, "standing up" rather than simply "standing by" and waiting for a situation to come to its natural conclusion. The question then is: How do we teach students to assert themselves when they witness issues of conflict, discord, bullying, or anger in the larger school dynamic?

- *Teach empathy:* Schools should provide lessons in classes and assemblies that encourage students to put themselves in someone else's shoes. Practical social skill opportunities should be included as a part of this curriculum. Finally, parenting programs should be implemented to teach parents to use and harness this vital skill at home as well. (More on how to get parents involved later in the chapter.)
- *Feed good behavior rather than bad behavior:* Bullying behavior tends to get a lot of attention from students and faculty alike. Faculty should provide consequences and attention to these behaviors, but with as little energy and emotion as possible. *This does not mean no consequences are applied!* On the contrary, it means that consequences are applied swiftly and appropriately, but that energy is reserved for the students whose behaviors deserve the full positive energy and attention of the educator. Students also should be encouraged not to glorify and publish when discord occurs, within the school or outside the school environment but to squelch it.

- *Find leadership:* As is true of adults, there are some children who are just naturally better leaders. These children tend to be more popular and have greater influence on their classmates than others in the student body. These pupils should be tapped as leaders to start an upstander movement, as they are generally the best advocates to speak to students and bring the message to them versus the adults who are deemed "outsiders" in the society of youth.
- *Teach those "I" messages:* Students should be taught to communicate with those who are sending inappropriate and harmful messages to others, addressing how it makes them feel, why they feel that way, and what they want or need the other peer to do to solve the issue. This provides children with a solid template for advocating for themselves as well as others.
- *Emphasize advocacy in the classroom*: Discuss people from history as well as in current events who advocate for the rights of others. Discuss empathy, how to advocate for the targets of bullying and intimidation, and how to apply these concepts to address problems in the larger school community.
- *Don't tolerate gossip*: Students can learn a lot from the wise mentor Sathya Sai Baba, who implored, "Before you speak, ask yourself, is it kind, is it necessary, is it true, does it improve the silence?" This can be a good formula that children can easily use to decrease both verbal and internet gossip. Additionally, even a simple game like Telephone can demonstrate firsthand the dangers of gossip. For those not familiar with this childhood game, children are challenged to whisper a complex statement from one to another and see how the words morph to something that is usually quite different from the original statement. This simple lesson can be extremely powerful for illustrating the viral nature of rumors.
- *Grant students permission to advocate:* Students are often fearful that they may do the wrong thing and get themselves into trouble. This applies to the uncharted waters of standing up for peers in challenging situations. A definitive means of determining what is acceptable in asserting themselves and where the limits are must be developed by students, teachers, and administrators and district policy makers alike.

- *Emphasize telling versus tattling:* As discussed in chapter 4, students must know that *telling* is an appropriate response to situations in which someone is hurt, in danger, or being bullied. These crucial issues require the assistance of an adult. Students should first attempt to deal with minor issues independently.

REFLECT ON EQ AS MUCH AS IQ

We often discuss the importance of children's intelligence quotient (IQ) in schools. It is how we organize them in class groupings, what we measure on standardized testing, and one of the primary factors we use in provision of special education. Yet we all know adults who have an incredibly high IQ but still miss vital social cues or lack particular social skills or abilities; this deficiency greatly limits their potential for success personally and socially.

With this in mind, it is just as important that we also teach around students' emotional intelligence (EQ), a concept popularized by Daniel Goleman, cofounder of the Collaborative for Academic, Social, and Emotional Learning, in his books and lectures.

The components of EQ include:

- *Self-awareness:* The ability to be aware of how you are feeling
- *Self-regulation:* The ability to control your own feelings and emotions
- *Internal motivation:* Mastery of priorities in determining what is important in your own life
- *Empathy:* Knowledge of understanding others' feelings and emotions
- *Social skills:* The aptitude and understanding of how to function in the various aspects of society, school, and the world in general

These EQ attributes foster kindness, teamwork, success, and self-esteem in their own right. Without these skills, students cannot acknowledge each other, work together, or develop the school climate necessary to snuff out anger and eventually become productive members of society.

How Do We Integrate EQ into Schools?

- *Start early and often:* The earlier we start, the more opportunity we have to sculpt children's emotional skill set and subsequent EQ. As young as preschool, we should begin to discuss feelings and integrate them into an understanding of how others feel. One way to do this is by discussing characters in books, surmising how the respective characters may feel. Thus, comprehension should be expanded past reading comprehension; it should include and encompass emotional comprehension as well.
- *Hold meetings with classes:* As the world of public education becomes ever more packed with requirements and standards, other aspects get pushed out (by necessity of time). Therefore, anything that is vital must be intentionally scheduled within the lesson plans of the day. Holding morning or afternoon meetings can provide an opportunity for teachers to mentor situations that students bring up as well as provide peer support regarding these concerns. It also allows students to feel that their teachers understand and respect the lives they have outside of the school day and their larger emotional development.
- *Teach conflict resolution skills:* Basic conflict resolution skills and role-playing are important parts of school and life. Some of these elements may seem to be common sense to adults; however, when children are enraged, an inability to use those skills without sufficient practice may ensue. Conflict resolution skills include:

  - Learning to apologize appropriately versus just making an empty, knee-jerk apology
  - Recognizing and accepting responsibility for what you are specifically responsible for
  - Learning that walking away does not equate to cowardice or losing in a situation
  - Understanding that asserting yourself means not only showing that you are angry, but also expressing what you specifically need or want to fix the problem
  - Learning to make a deal that allows everyone to get some of what they want, but no one gets everything

- *Teach mindfulness and kindness:* Nothing destroys empathy and school climate faster than unbridled anger and rage. Anger can develop from a mixture of emotions, such as fear, anxiety, sadness, or jealousy. Mindfulness is an effective way to alleviate these harmful emotions. Teaching mindfulness is, quite simply—and challengingly—teaching students that their feelings and emotions can be separated from their actions and identity and to deal with the moment versus the burden of the past or worry of the future.
- *Showing empathy:* If the faculty as a whole does not demonstrate empathy toward each other and toward students, you are not providing a vital and necessary model for students to learn to do so.
- *Use writing for self-reflection:* We often require children to write about various subjects, stories, and people. Yet teaching them to write about themselves and their feelings may, in fact, be the most useful life skill to learn as the authors of their own life stories. Journaling can be a very therapeutic and necessary activity from a number of avenues.
- *Foster an understanding of feelings:* When most children are asked how they feel, the response is generally "good" or "okay." Yet we know that feelings are not that simple or black and white. There are many degrees and colors of emotions in the palette of feelings. Reviewing these each day helps students to better pinpoint the range of emotions that exist and allows them to expand their vocabulary in this area. (As a teaching aid, many posters of youth demonstrating the range of feelings are available online or for purchase.)
- *Offer specific praise:* Specifically telling students what you like about a behavior encourages that behavior to be repeated again. For instance, instead of saying, "Good job," clarify what a "good job" looks like, with specific behavioral indicators.
- *Say "Do" instead of "Don't":* Many times, we lean toward telling students what *not* to do rather than telling them what they *should* do. This assumes that students can understand what to do because we have described what behaviors they are *not* supposed to engage in. It is better to give them information about what you want them to do than to leave them to try to "fill in the blanks" in this area.

INCLUDE PARENTS IN PROGRAMS

It is vital to remember that students are only in school for six hours per day. The other eighteen hours are generally at home (if not in before- or after-school care). Hence, it is vital that a connection is made between parents and school whenever possible. Parent enrichment programs can teach parents how to help their children deal with anger by employing appropriate disciplinary skills. These programs can also provide intervention and a further connection between home and school.

One of the primary frustrations that educators face, however, is that the students with the most anger and disciplinary issues generally have the parents who seem least involved. Reciprocally, those who generally have significantly fewer issues are those whose parents are most present and are likely to be at these very programs.

The following are some ideas for getting those at-risk parents to attend parental enrichment programs.

- *Don't expect them to come to you:* Parents of children with anger or other issues simply may not be able to come to you for a host of reasons (i.e., being overwhelmed, finances, transportation). Target where your at-risk students are and hold the programs at those locations. Often you can find a condo or apartment complex clubhouse or a community center to give you the space at no cost if you can help them see that the benefit of improved parenting skills will systematically improve quality-of-life issues within the neighborhood.
- *Provide dinner:* Nothing draws people like food. As families struggle for money and time, one dinner that they do not have to buy and prepare is a great relief to their pocketbooks and schedules. Attendance may also be better near the end of a month, when food stamps may be exhausted. Additionally, many chain restaurants have a budget allotted to help the community by providing food. Another option is to request that these restaurants offer food donations in exchange for free advertising by the PTA, PTO, or the like.
- *Involve children and parents at the same time:* When you have children at your events, parents will typically trail not too far behind. If you can encourage the children to be excited about the

event, you just have to schedule your parent enrichment program and both will likely show up.

- *Choose topics that are long on practicality and short on theory:* Parents who are struggling urgently need someone to throw them a life preserver. Keep the topics current and address only the most practical topics. Break the subject areas down so they can be reviewed in one night (e.g., "How to Deal with Temper Tantrums" or "How to Get Your Child to Listen"). Avoid program titles that are too vague, such as "Family Communication," as these will generally not generate as much interest.

- *Focus on other resources, too:* Most at-risk parents are dealing with difficult issues such as unemployment, illness, abuse, and so on. If possible, ask representatives from local social services agencies to be present so they can answer questions and distribute appropriate materials.

- *Be effective in your advertising:* When a flier comes home with a child, it usually ends up in the circular file, so you need to work harder to spread the word. Find out where the parents you want to participate are most likely to see your fliers (e.g., community centers or grocery stores). The most viable action is to simply make personal phone calls or send e-mails to the parents you want there. Of course, you should use your school website and social media to advertise these events as well. Will this take more time? Yes, but it is vastly better than wasting your time presenting a program to a roomful of empty chairs. Another effective way to publicize your program is to ask those who found it useful to spread the information by word of mouth.

- *Focus on fun:* Create an icebreaker and parent-child activities that help foster bonding and enjoyment. Make it a memorable time for everyone involved.

- *Include the teachers:* Have teachers provide incentives in their classes (i.e., homework passes) for students who attend with their parents. Having teachers present at these events also lets parents and students see that the faculty are part of a team in the students' development.

- *Give things away:* Review your district's policies about this first. sometimes the PTA/PTO can help with door prizes or other freebies that parents and children can take home.

- *Throw away the RSVP:* Most parents who have a lot on their plates are not going to respond, so don't make it a requirement.
- *Remember that less is more:* Focus on quality over quantity. Make the program no more than an hour, but remember to leave time for a question-and-answer period, as this provides an opportunity for parents to support each other.
- *Just say thanks:* Provide a sign-in sheet so you can call and personally thank the parents who attended. This is a little gesture that means a lot. You can also use this list to call these specific parents when promoting the next program session.
- *Don't take this for granted:* Grants can generate necessary funding for parent programs. If your district has a designated grant writer, this person may be a helpful resource.
- *Always offer encouragement:* It goes without saying that parental programs should be kept positive. Parents who have challenging children may already feel guilty, judged, and frustrated. Let the parents know that your goal is to enrich, not criticize or change, who they are or what they do as parents. Many families have had bad experiences with schools, child protective services, or other agencies or institutions. Don't turn them away by criticizing the job they are doing. Most parents are doing the best they can with what they have.
- *Notify social service programs and agencies:* If you know of private counselors or social service agencies that provide for students or families, have them encourage parents to participate in your programs. This is an opportunity for them to advertise and for parents to learn from their expertise. It is a win/win for both parties.

NOTES

1. THE STORM ON THE HORIZON

1. Meghan Neal, "1 in 12 Teens Has 'Anger Disorder': Study," *New York Daily News*, April 9, 2018, http://www.nydailynews.com/news/national/1–12-teens-anger-disorder-study-article-1.1108696.

2. Mental Health Foundation, *Boiling Point: Problem Anger and What We Can Do About It* (London: Mental Health Foundation, n.d.), http://www.mentalhealth.org.uk/sites/default/files/boilingpoint.pdf.

3. Brian Fung, "The Internet Isn't Making Us Dumb. It's Making Us Angry," *Washington Post*, September 16, 2013, http://www.washingtonpost.com/news/the-switch/wp/2013/09/16/the-internet-isnt-making-us-dumb-its-making-us-angry.

4. Jeff Thompson, "Is Nonverbal Communication a Numbers Game?" *Psychology Today*, September 30, 2011, http://www.psychologytoday.com/us/blog/beyond-words/201109/is-nonverbal-communication-numbers-game.

5. Anderson, Mae. "AP-NORC Poll: For Many Online Americans, Facebook is a Habit." AP NEWS, Associated Press, 24 Apr. 2018, https://www.apnews.com/e74d3e9a947645df8fabbd68a8440a9a.

6. Lindfors, Pirjo L., et al. "Cyberbullying among Finnish Adolescents—a Population-Based Study." BMC Public Health, BioMed Central, 23 Nov. 2012, https://www.ncbi.nlm.nih.gov/pmc/articles/PMC3585473/.

7. "One in Five Young People Lose Sleep over Social Media." *Science-Daily*, January 16, 2017, www.sciencedaily.com/releases/2017/01/170116091419.html.

8. Vanessa Chalmers, "Losing Just Two Hours of Sleep Makes You ANGRIER: Study Uncovers the First Proof between Irritability and a Lack of

Shut-Eye," *Daily Mail Online*, November 29, 2018, http://www.dailymail.co.uk/health/article-6441687/Losing-just-two-hours-sleep-makes-ANGRIER.html.

9. Marianne Schmid Mast and William Ickes, "Empathic Accuracy: Measurement and Potential Clinical Applications," 408–27, in *Empathy in Mental Illness*, ed. T. F. D. Farrow and P. W. R. Woodruff (Cambridge: Cambridge University Press, 2007), DOI: 10.1017/CBO9780511543753.023.

10. Teresa Amabile and Steven Kramer, "Inner Work Life: Understanding the Subtext of Business Performance," *IEEE Engineering Management Review* 43, no. 1 (2015): 43–51, DOI: 10.1109/emr.2015.7059374.

11. Patricia Arriaga et al., "Effects of Playing Violent Computer Games on Emotional Desensitization and Aggressive Behavior," *Journal of Applied Social Psychology* 41, no. 8 (2011): 1900–25, DOI: 10.1111/j.1559–1816.2011.00791.x.

12. Anderson, Craig A., and Brad J. Bushman. "Effects of Violent Video Games on Aggressive Behavior, Aggressive Cognition, Aggressive Affect, Physiological Arousal, and Prosocial Behavior: A Meta-Analytic Review of the Scientific Literature—Craig A. Anderson, Brad J. Bushman, 2001." Sage Journals, https://journals.sagepub.com/do1/abs/10.111/1467-9280.00366.

13. Dr. Neil, MD, "The Fight or Flight Response," http://www.thebodysoulconnection.com/EducationCenter/fight.html.

14. "University of Iowa Study: ADHD Rates in US Children Rising Sharply," *Trial Site News*, September 1, 2018, http://www.trialsitenews.com/university-of-iowa-study-adhd-rates-in-us-children-rising-sharply.

15. Fiza Pirani, "Perfectionism Is a Major Issue for Millennials and Their Mental Health, Study Says," *Atlanta Journal-Constitution*, October 10, 2018, http://www.ajc.com/news/health-med-fit-science/perfectionism-major-issue-for-millennials-and-their-mental-health-study-says/I8kLLVynVamx8hcseUW6wK.

16. Jean Twenge, "With Teen Mental Health Deteriorating over Five Years, There's a Likely Culprit," *The Conversation*, November 14, 2017, http://www.theconversation.com/with-teen-mental-health-deteriorating-over-five-years-theres-a-likely-culprit-86996.

2. PARENTING THE ANGRY CHILD

1. "CDC's Development Milestones | CDC." Centers for Disease Control and Prevention, https://www.cdc.gov/ncbddd/actearly/milestones/index.html.

2. Liraz Margalit, "The Psychology of Choice," *Psychology Today*, October 3, 2014, www.psychologytoday.com/us/blog/behind-online-behavior/201410/the-psychology-choice.

3. IT IS NO ONE'S FAULT

1. "Jean M. Twenge Quotes (Author of Generation Me)." Goodreads, https://www.goodreads.com/author/quotes/300231.Jean_M_Twenge.
2. Adam Davidson, "It's Official: The Boomerang Kids Won't Leave," *New York Times*, June 20, 2014, www.nytimes.com/2014/06/22/magazine/its-official-the-boomerang-kids-wont-leave.html.

4. THE REVOLUTION OF CONFLICT RESOLUTION

1. Crocker, Lester G. *The Age of Enlightenment.* Harper & Row, 1969.
2. "Laurence J. Peter Quotes." *BrainyQuote*, Xplore, https://www.brainyquote.com/authors/laurence_j_peter.

5. THE MATCH

1. "Understanding the Stress Response," *Harvard Health Blog*, May 1, 2018, www.health.harvard.edu/staying-healthy/understanding-the-stress-response.
2. McCahill, Laurence. "Easy Steps for (Incredible) Focus—Tips from Danial Goleman [EXCLUSIVE INTERVIEW]." ShamashaAlidina.com, 5 Dec. 2013, https://www.shamashalidina.com/blog/easy-steps-for-focus-tips-from-daniel-goleman.

6. A KINDER, GENTLER SCHOOL

1. David W. Johnson and Roger T. Johnson, *Reducing School Violence through Conflict Resolution* (Alexandria, VA: Association for Supervision and Curriculum Development, 1995). pg. 2–3.
2. iResearchNet, "Bystander Effect," psychology.iresearchnet.com/social-psychology/prosocial-behavior/bystander-effect.

3. "Bystander Effect," *Psychology Today*, www.psychologytoday.com/us/basics/bystander-effect.

4. J. M. Darley and B. Latane, *The Unresponsive Bystander: Why Doesn't He Help?* (New York: Appleton Century Crofts, 1970).

INDEX

ABOUT THE AUTHOR

Brett Novick holds a bachelor's degree in psychology from LaSalle University in Philadelphia and a master's degree in family therapy from Friends University in Wichita, Kansas. He has also done postgraduate degree work and certification in school social work at Monmouth University in West Long Branch, New Jersey, as well as postgraduate certification in educational leadership. He is licensed as a marriage and family therapist and state certified as a school social worker, supervisor, principal, and educational administrator.

He has worked as a school social worker/counselor for the last nineteen years and is an adjunct instructor at Rutgers University in New Brunswick, New Jersey. Additionally, he has been a licensed marriage and family therapist in private practice, community mental health, and substance abuse settings over the past twenty years. He has supervised in family counseling, school counseling, and centers for abused and neglected children as well as for adults and children with developmental disabilities.

He has also authored articles in *American Association of Marriage and Family Therapy*, *Autism Parenting*, *National Education Digest*, *NJEA Review*, *National Association of Special Education Teachers*, *NASSP Principal Leadership*, *Better Mental Health*, and *ASCD Educational Leadership*. He has authored six other books: *Beyond the Behavior Contract*, *Parents and Teachers Working Together*, and the *Likeable, Effective, and Productive Educator*, published by Rowman & Littlefield; *Don't Marry a Lemon* and *Crappy to Happy*, published by

Train of Thought Press; and *Brain Bullies: Standing Up to Anxiety and Worry*, published through Childswork/Childsplay.

He has been humbled with numerous awards for his work in education, inclusive education, counseling, character education, and human rights. These accolades include the New Jersey Governor's Jefferson Award for Public Service, the NJEA Martin Luther King Jr. Human and Civil Rights Award, the NJSCA Ocean County School Counselor of the Year Award, the Ocean County Mental Health Advocate Award, the New Jersey Council on Developmental Disabilities Community Award, the New Jersey Department of Education Holocaust Educator Hela Young Award, the New Jersey Department of Education Exemplary Educator Award, the NJSCA Human Rights Advocate Award, the ETS/Kids Bridge Character Educator of the Year Award, and US Congressional Recognition for Community Service.